Instructor's Resource Manual for

Technical Communication

Instructor's Resource Manual for

Seventh Edition

Technical Communication

Mike Markel
Boise State University

Bedford/St. Martin's
Boston • New York

Manufactured in the United States of America.

8 7 6 5 4
f e d c b a

For information, write:
Bedford/St. Martin's
75 Arlington Street, Boston, MA 02116
(617-399-4000)

ISBN: 0-312-40929-X

How to Use This *Instructor's Resource Manual*

The purpose of this *Instructor's Resource Manual* is to help instructors use *Technical Communication,* Seventh Edition, and TechComm Web, its integrated companion Web site, successfully. The *Instructor's Resource Manual* consists of four parts:

1. *Teaching Topics.* These brief essays discuss issues important to tech-comm teachers. Teaching Topics present concise, classroom-tested advice and techniques for creating a positive atmosphere for teaching. Each Teaching Topic provides links to other resources on the Internet for further study. (The Teaching Topics are also presented on the Instructor Resources section of TechComm Web <bedfordstmartins.com/techcomm>).
   - "Making the Transition from Comp to Tech Comm." Explains the continuity between composition and tech comm and suggests resources instructors might consult to learn more about technical communication.
   - "Addressing Plagiarism in the Tech-Comm Course." Focuses on techniques for preventing and detecting plagiarism and crafting assignments that discourage plagiarism.
   - "Integrating Technology in the Tech-Comm Course." Explains how to decide what technology skills you wish your students to acquire in the course and suggests ways to integrate those skills into your assignments.
   - "Teaching Distance Education with *Technical Communication.*" Explains how to use the text effectively in the distance classroom.
2. *Major Features of* Technical Communication *and TechComm Web.* This section provides a brief overview of the contents of the text and the companion site, TechComm Web, as well as suggestions about how to use these integrated resources effectively in the classroom.
3. *Sample Syllabus and Schedules.* This section describes how to find Mike Markel's downloadable syllabus online. In addition, it presents five schedules, each with a different focus, that you can adapt to meet your own objectives and your students' needs.
4. *Chapter-by-Chapter Guide to* Technical Communication. For each chapter, this section provides a summary, teaching goals, teaching tips for both traditional and computerized classrooms, and suggestions for responding to every Interactive Sample Document, exercise, project, and case in the book.

Contents

1. Teaching Topics

The four brief essays included in this section may also be downloaded from the Instructor Resources section of TechComm Web <bedfordstmartins.com/techcomm>.

Making the Transition from Comp to Tech Comm

by Mike Markel

Technical communication is not a strange and exotic form of encryption; it is simply another kind of composition. It follows, then, that technical communication and composition share the same foundation: rhetoric. The skills and experiences you have acquired as a teacher of composition are the best preparation for a successful, rewarding experience in the tech-comm classroom.

This Teaching Topic is meant to help you make the transition from teaching comp to teaching tech comm. It consists of four sections:

- who takes the course, and why
- major similarities and differences between comp and tech comm
- understanding the technical subjects students write about
- resources that will help you learn more about tech comm

Who Takes Tech Comm, and Why

Most tech-comm students are somewhat older, more experienced, and more capable than first-year students. They are likely to have taken some courses in their major. Although many students are required to take tech comm, many other students take it as an elective because they understand that tech comm is the kind of writing they will be doing in the workplace. For this reason, student motivation tends to be higher in tech comm than in the typical first-year comp class. In the 30 years I have taught this course, I have *never* had a student who questioned the value of studying the subject.

Students are eager to learn practical skills. They want to be able to communicate more effectively in their other courses and on the job. They want to write more quickly, and they want their readers to understand the information more easily. They want practice writing memos, e-mails, letters, reports, instructions, and Web sites, and they want to learn how to deliver oral presentations.

Major Similarities and Differences between Comp and Tech Comm

As you review *Technical Communication* and its companion site, TechComm Web <bedfordstmartins.com/techcomm>, you will see that you can use the same basic approach that you have used in your comp courses. Teaching tech comm calls for the process approach; for invention techniques such as freewriting and heuristics such as the journalistic questions; for peer-editing and collaboration; and for revising a document thoroughly to make sure it responds to the needs of the audience and is true to the subject.

In addition, both comp and tech comm are essentially rhetorical. Both are based on the premise that communication is addressed to an audience and intended to fulfill a purpose. Just as a comp assignment might call for students to write an op-ed piece for the student newspaper to argue for a change in academic policies, an assignment in tech comm might call for students to write a report to their major department calling for a revision to the requirements to complete the major.

Both comp and tech comm focus on persuasion. Chapter 6 of *Technical Communication* discusses techniques of understanding the audience's goals, finding appropriate kinds of evidence, considering opposing viewpoints, and organizing the argument. In addition, it covers logical fallacies, the use of graphics in persuasion, and the challenges of writing persuasive messages to multicultural audiences. In writing this chapter, I have deliberately drawn on the concepts presented in the leading comp texts because I believe that the best way to help students (and instructors) make the transition from comp to tech comm is to help them see the continuity between the two types of writing.

Although comp and tech comm are both process-based and essentially rhetorical, there are two main differences in emphasis:

- *Tech comm uses more technology.* Although many comp courses today are quite high-tech, tech comm often leads composition in the use of technology. You will probably want to teach your students to use the outline view in their word processing software as an aid in planning a document, as well as how to use the reviewing and commenting features as an aid in collaboration; you will want to teach them how to write effective e-mails, how to use the Web as a research tool, how to use Web boards to find job openings, and how to write scannable résumés; and you might want to teach your students how to design and create basic Web sites. The Teaching Topic "Integrating Technology in the Tech-Comm Course" goes into more detail on this aspect of the course.
- *Tech comm focuses more on product: the size and shape of the finished document.* Whereas the finished product in a comp course is often an essay, the products of a tech-comm course are more likely to have counterparts in today's working world: sets of instructions, e-mails, reports, and so forth. And these documents are likely to be formatted to include multiple columns, headings, bulleted lists, and figures and tables. To say that tech-comm documents are formatted, however, does not mean that you are teaching students to do cookie-cutter writing. Fundamental to any tech-comm course is the idea that writers need to learn how to adapt to the rhetorical context, including audience, subject, and purpose. This adaptation often calls for breaking the mold.

Understanding the Technical Subjects Students Write About

Although understanding technical subjects is a common concern for new teachers of tech comm, in fact it's not likely to be a problem. For one thing, most students in the basic tech-comm course are not writing about highly technical subjects. Students are much more likely to be writing about which sport-utility vehicle a company ought to purchase for its fleet than about some arcane aspect of particle physics.

For another thing, the focus of the course is not the details of the technical subject but the rhetoric of the text the student creates about the subject. You can read the document and comment on it constructively even if you don't understand all the details. What you will be looking for—organization, structure, style, and so forth—will be easy enough to evaluate even if you don't follow all the details.

Resources That Will Help You Learn More about Tech Comm

Listed here are some organizations, journals, and conferences that can be of value to you as a teacher of technical communication:

- **The Association of Teachers of Technical Writing (ATTW)** <www.attw.org> links to numerous resources, including its quarterly journal, *The Technical Communication Quarterly,* and a semiannual *Bulletin.* ATTW sponsors an e-mail discussion list,

ATTW-L. The Web site links to a collection of course syllabi on many different topics in technical communication, as well as other valuable resources. ATTW also has an active publications program, including the ATTW Contemporary Studies in Technical Communication, annual bibliographies, and books on pedagogical issues. The association also sponsors an annual convention.

- **The Society for Technical Communication (STC)** <www.stc.org> publishes a quarterly journal, *Technical Communication,* containing articles about all aspects of technical communication for both the instructor and the professional, as well as a bibliography of recent articles and reviews of recent books and texts. STC also publishes the newsletter *Intercom* 10 times a year. Membership in STC also carries membership in a regional STC branch. Most branches meet monthly, and there are regional and international conferences.
- **The Institute of Electrical and Electronics Engineers, Inc. (IEEE),** Professional Communication Society <www.ieeepcs.org>, publishes *IEEE Transactions on Professional Communication,* a quarterly, which contains many useful articles for the technical-communication instructor, as well as a newsletter. The Professional Communication Society sponsors an annual international conference.
- ***The Journal of Technical Writing and Communication,*** published by Baywood Publishing Company <www.baywood.com>, is an excellent source of research articles. Baywood also publishes a highly regarded book series on tech comm.
- ***Journal of Business and Technical Communication,*** published by Sage Publications <www.sagepub.com>, publishes research and pedagogical articles.
- **Short courses on tech comm.** There are short courses on tech comm held in the summer, including the Technical Writers' Institute held at Rensselaer Polytechnic Institute, Communicating Technical Information at MIT, and Teaching Technical and Professional Writing at the University of Michigan. Contact the continuing-education divisions or convention bureaus at these institutions for information.

Addressing Plagiarism in the Tech-Comm Course

by Roger Munger

Plagiarism is the use of another's work or ideas without acknowledgment. Students knowingly and unknowingly plagiarize assignments, and the exact number of students who plagiarize is significantly higher than most instructors believe. In this article, I briefly discuss the major issues plagiarism presents to instructors and then offer some specific strategies for preventing and detecting plagiarism in your technical communication course. Finally, I present a list of helpful online resources.

Forms of Plagiarism

Perhaps the most common form of plagiarism occurs when students turn in assignments that have been previously submitted by other students. The longer you teach your course and use the same assignments, the greater the odds are that students will be able to gain access to old assignments. Many student organizations such as dormitories, fraternities, and sororities keep paper and digital files of assignments and tests completed by their members.

In recent years, the anonymity and ease of access provided by the Internet has made plagiarism very tempting to some students. Students can insert passages of information found on various Web sites and pass them off as their own work. For example, in a mechanism description on scanners, a student might cut and paste passages from product descriptions found at manufacturer sites or information from sites such as HowStuffWorks.com <www.howstuffworks.com>. Because of the nature of tech-comm assignments, some students will be tempted to cut and paste graphics, icons, logos, data sets, and source code (for example, HTML, XHTML, and JavaScript) without acknowledging the original creators.

Digital term-paper mills, like their paper-based counterparts, supply students with ready-to-submit papers on a variety of technical topics. All seem to operate on the concept "Download Your Workload," as one Web site proclaims. With more and more colleges offering tech-comm courses and degrees, the demand for pre-written technical communication assignments will continue to increase. Although these sites do not currently offer a huge selection of ready-to-submit papers specifically for tech-comm courses, digital paper mills in time will certainly come to recognize tech-comm assignments as another lure to unscrupulous students.

In short, some students—perhaps more than you imagine—will be tempted to plagiarize their responses to some or all of your assignments. Moreover, the Internet makes plagiarism quick, cheap, and anonymous. However, the same speed and reach capabilities that make the Internet a tempting tool for dishonest students also make it an excellent tool for you to prevent and detect plagiarism in your course.

Strategies for Preventing Plagiarism

Your best strategy for combating plagiarism is to stop it before it starts. Following are eight strategies you can use to prevent plagiarism.

1. Openly discuss plagiarism, your school's honor code, and digital paper mills. By spending class time on these topics, you demonstrate to your students that you are serious about academic honesty, on the lookout for plagiarism in your course, and aware of the ways dishonest students try to get out of doing work.
2. Ask students to commit to adhering to your school's honor code. At the start of the semester, ask students to read a policy statement printed in or linked to your syl-

labus and then e-mail you a statement acknowledging their understanding of the policy and its consequences and agreeing to adhere to it.

3. Do not assume that students understand the concept of plagiarism or documenting sources. Explain how to appropriately integrate other people's ideas in documents and how to accurately identify the source of the ideas.
4. Keep a list of report topics and project titles from past courses. If other instructors in your department teach similar courses, keep an updated master list and distribute it at the start of each semester. Just knowing that you keep track of such things will help deter students from plagiarizing past assignments.
5. Design your assignments so that generic responses will not work. You can make an assignment specific to your course by including a detailed description of the audience, context, and purpose. You can also require students to use specific data sets, resource materials, or design features.
6. Take an active role in the writing process. Ask students to submit in-class work, rough drafts, and progress reports before they submit final documents. You can also meet with students to discuss their projects.
7. Ask students to attach to their assignments a short memo describing the audience and purpose of the document they created and their design choices. You might also ask them to assess the strengths and weaknesses of their effort.
8. Periodically change your assignments. The tech-comm profession changes rapidly in response to changes in communication technologies and business practices. Every so often, you should revise your assignments or create new ones to reflect current practices in the profession and to prevent students from recycling responses.

Strategies for Detecting Plagiarism

If you suspect that a student is guilty of plagiarism, the following strategies might help you build your case. Often merely talking to a student and raising your concerns about plagiarism will be enough to elicit a confession or make the student aware that he or she might have unknowingly plagiarized. However, to avoid false accusations and to convince more hardened students, you will need to find proof. Following are seven strategies you can use to detect plagiarism.

1. Look for inconsistencies in diction, style, and tone. Such inconsistencies might indicate cut-and-paste plagiarism. In addition, look for obvious giveaways such as incorrect dates (for example, a report dated June 1, 1997, for an assignment due in 2003) and references (for example, quotes from interviews) to people whom your students are unlikely to know.
2. Compare in-class writing to assignments created outside of class for significant differences in writing ability. Although an in-class writing assignment will be less polished than one created outside of class, significant differences in diction, tone, and style might indicate plagiarism.
3. Look for extraneous material or awkward responses to your assignment. Although such flaws might suggest that a student is short on time or is struggling to master a new writing style, they might also indicate that he or she is trying to fit a generic paper purchased from a paper mill or submitted in another course to your specific assignment requirements.
4. Use search engines such as Google <www.google.com> to search for distinctive phrases or images from the student's submitted work. Because each search engine's database is different, try more than one search engine.
5. For student-created Web pages, view the source code in addition to searching the text and images. Use your Web browser's view-source feature to look for evidence left by the original author such as his or her name or comments.

6. Find likely sources of information by performing a subject search (for example, *scanners*) at sites such as Yahoo! <www.yahoo.com>. Many students in a hurry will plagiarize information from the first sites listed in the search results.
7. Consider using an Internet-based detection service to check for plagiarism. At present, these services work best for detecting plagiarized text. Most cannot handle highly formatted documents such as instructions, graphics, or Web sites. You can find detection services by searching the Internet for *plagiarism detection*.

Online Resources on Plagiarism

Plagiarism and Honor
<www.english.vt.edu/%7EIDLE/plagiarism/plagiarism1.html>
A seven-part module on plagiarism and honor developed by Cheryl Ruggiero of the Virginia Tech Department of English. Although designed for Virginia Tech students, modules 1 through 3 are applicable to most courses.

Avoiding Plagiarism
<owl.english.purdue.edu/handouts/research/r_plagiar.html>
A resource designed for students by Purdue University's Online Writing Lab. The handout is available online in printer-friendly format and as a PDF file.

Plagiarized.com
<www.plagiarized.com/index.shtml>
This site provides advice, articles, online training, and sample papers.

Internet Paper Mills
<www.coastal.edu/library/mills2.htm>
An extensive and recently updated list of over 250 Internet paper mills compiled by Margaret Fain of Coastal Carolina University. Use this resource both to openly discuss Internet paper mills with your students and to detect possible instances of plagiarism.

Plagiarism and the Internet
<www.oucs.ox.ac.uk/ltg/reports/plag.shtml>
A detailed report on strategies and resources for dealing with plagiarism associated with the Internet.

Anti-Plagiarism Strategies for Research Papers
<www.virtualsalt.com/antiplag.htm>
This detailed article by Robert Harris, author of *The Plagiarism Handbook* (Pyrczak, 2001), offers insight into why students cheat, strategies for prevention, and strategies for detection.

The Bedford/St. Martin's Workshop on Plagiarism
<bcs.bedfordstmartins.com/plagiarism/default.asp>
This online faculty workshop on preventing and detecting plagiarism includes printable handouts and links to related resources.

Integrating Technology in the Tech-Comm Course

by Roger Munger

New technologies affect the way people plan, write, design, and produce technical communication. In fact, a person's skills in using existing technology and in quickly learning new technology are important factors in many hiring and promotion decisions. As a teacher of technical communication, you will want to decide on the role technology will play in your course.

You probably already have an idea of the rhetorical goals for your course and the major assignments. A broad rhetorical goal for a tech comm class might be the following: "Students will create a variety of workplace documents that help a specific audience accomplish a task, solve a problem, or understand a subject." For a specific assignment, you might want students to be able to write a clear, concise, and accurate mechanism description. But you will also want to answer this question: What technology skills do I want my students to possess at the end of my course?

Of course, there is no one right answer to this question. Your answer will depend on factors such as your own technology skills, your students' technology skills, the course-delivery method (for example, face-to-face instruction, traditional classroom, computer lab, or online), and students' access to technology. Your answer will also depend on how much of a role you want technology to play in your day-to-day class activities.

Below I discuss four topics: techniques for finding resources about technology, core skills in technology, approaches to teaching technology skills, and strategies for evaluating your students' technology skills. Throughout I include links to online resources, references to chapters in *Technical Communication,* and resources available on the book companion site, TechComm Web <bedfordstmartins.com/techcomm>.

Techniques for Finding Resources about Technology
To find resources for yourself and your students, consider these techniques:

1. Consult the online help included with software applications.
2. Read print guides (for example, *Visual Quickstart Guides, Teach Yourself in 24 Hours,* and *Classroom in a Book* series) available at libraries and bookstores.
3. Investigate the resources or training offered through your school's library or instructional-technology service.
4. Use search engines (see Chapter 7) to find online resources. You can find online tutorials by searching a manufacturer's Web site (for example, Microsoft in Education <www.microsoft.com/education/?ID=Tutorials>). You can find additional tutorials and resources by searching the Web using an application's name and version, the word *tutorial,* and a keyword (for example, *Excel 97* and *tutorial* and *charts*). Mac users will also want to include *Mac* in their queries.

Because different versions of an application can differ significantly in terms of screen layout and features, check that a resource is appropriate for the software version (for example, Microsoft Office 2000 vs. XP) and platform (PC or Mac) to which you and your students will have access.

Core Skills in Technology

When deciding which technology skills to teach in your course, start by examining your course's rhetorical goals. Then decide which technology skills your students will need to successfully meet those rhetorical goals. Following is a ranked list of core skills for you to consider for your own course.

1. **E-mail**
   a. Sending and retrieving messages, including creating distribution lists (for example, sending a message to all members of a project).
   b. Attaching files to messages.
   c. Following e-mail etiquette. See Chapter 15 as well as E-mailreplies.com <www.e-mailreplies.com/>.
2. **World Wide Web**
   a. Using search engines to locate information. See Chapter 7 and Search Engine Watch <www.searchenginewatch.com/>.
   b. Evaluating information found on the Web. See the tutorial "Evaluating Online Sources" in the Student Resources section of TechComm Web.
   c. Opening and printing PDF (portable document format) files from Web sites. A PDF file embeds all the fonts, layout elements, images, and other information needed to view and print a document. To open and print a PDF file, your students need Adobe Acrobat Reader, which they may download for free from <www.adobe.com/products/acrobat/readermain.html>.
   d. Capturing images on the Web. Images can be saved by placing your cursor over an image and using your browser's "save picture as" feature. You can capture entire screens and paste them into other documents. In addition, specialized programs for capturing screen images are also available; search the Internet for *screen capture programs*. Before your students copy material from the Web, they should understand their academic, ethical, and legal obligations (see Chapter 2 in the text and the Teaching Topic "Addressing Plagiarism in the Tech-Comm Course" in this manual).
3. **Word Processing**
   a. Designing a document by using a word processor's built-in style and formatting features. At a minimum, students should know how to use styles, columns, different kinds of tabs, page and section breaks, and headers and footers. See the tutorial "Designing Documents with a Word Processor" on TechComm Web and Florida Gulf Coast University's Styles Tutorial for Word 2000 <www.fgcu.edu/support/office2000/word/styles.html>.
   b. Understanding the uses and limitations of spell checkers, grammar checkers, and thesauri. See Chapter 3.
   c. Inserting and formatting tables. See Chapter 14.
   d. Using the Drawing and Picture toolbars to insert and modify graphics. For instance, students should be able to create a text box (for example, a box with a warning), insert a callout, use text wrapping, and crop images. See Florida Gulf Coast University's Graphics Tutorial for Word 2000 <www.fgcu.edu/support/office2000/word/graphics.html>.
   e. Using the comment, revision, and highlighting features. See Chapter 4.
4. **Spreadsheet Graphics**
   a. Entering numeric data in a spreadsheet.
   b. Portraying data in various kinds of graphics and charts. See, for example, Excel 97 Emphasizing Your Points with Charts Tutorial <www.microsoft.com/education/tutorial/classroom/excel97/chart.asp>.

c. Understanding basic design principles and how they are used in various kinds of graphics. See Chapter 14.
d. Understanding how to include spreadsheet-generated graphics in other applications such as word processing and presentation programs. See, for example, Florida Gulf Coast University's Graphics Tutorial for Excel 2000 <www.fgcu.edu/support/office2000/excel/charts.html>.

5. **Presentation Graphics**
   a. Selecting and modifying a slide's design and layout. See the tutorial "Preparing Presentation Slides" on TechComm Web, as well as Chapter 22 in the text.
   b. Importing and modifying graphics. See Florida Gulf Coast University's Graphics Tutorial for Word 2000 <www.fgcu.edu/support/office2000/word/graphics.html>.
   c. Producing slides, handouts, and notes. See the University of Rhode Island's PowerPoint® Tutorial <www.homepage.cs.uri.edu/tutorials/csc101/powerpoint/ppt.html>.

Approaches to Teaching Technology Skills

Although a lack of resources might prevent you from using one particular approach, you will likely have other options. Following are seven approaches to teaching core technology skills that you can adapt to meet the needs of your course.

1. **Demonstration.** Use a laptop and a data projector to demonstrate a technology skill. Many schools and departments allow instructors to borrow such equipment. A low-tech alternative: use transparencies of screen captures to show the layout of important screens and the location of menu options within a software application.
2. **Online and Print Help.** Direct students to read the online help available in an application. Begin your lesson by teaching students how to use the help's search features such as *index, answer wizard,* and *contents*. You can also make print help available as a class handout or place copies on reserve in your library. (Check your library's guidelines if you use copyrighted material.)
3. **Collaboration.** Ask students who already know a particular technology skill to help other students (and you).
4. **Expert Assistance.** If you do not know a particular skill, consider asking a colleague to visit your class and present the material, or take your class to a technology workshop offered elsewhere on campus. Your school's library and instructional-technology service might offer such guest lecturers and workshops.
5. **Drop-in Labs.** Many schools have drop-in labs open during the week and on weekends. Often these labs are staffed by people with expertise in common software applications. Although you do not want to send your entire class to a lab and expect a lab monitor to teach them the skills they need, many lab monitors can supply on-the-spot assistance as students work on a project. Also consider reserving a lab and holding class there.
6. **Web-based Tutorials.** Direct students to the tutorials provided on TechComm Web, the additional online tutorials discussed in this article, and to others you discover on the Web. Web-based tutorials serve as an excellent starting point for in-class discussions and practice using an application.
7. **Homework.** To reinforce class exercises, assign homework that requires students to practice relevant technology skills. For example, to help reinforce how to use a spreadsheet application to create graphics, you could supply students with a simple data set and ask them to use the application to create a chart based on the data.

Strategies for Evaluation

Following are four methods of evaluating how well individual students have learned technology skills in your course.

1. **Ask for electronic files of print work.** When looking at a print document, sometimes you cannot evaluate the methods or techniques a student used to create the finished work—for example, whether a student used a word processor's styles feature or merely formatted every heading individually. Ask your students to submit (on disk or to a server) the files from which the paper copies were printed. You can check the files to see if students are effectively using the software application.
2. **Assign in-class and homework exercises that require technology skills.** For example, ask students to send you a document as an attachment to an e-mail message or ask students to format a document as a two-column document with a header and a text box. When you collect these exercises, you can quickly see whether your students know these skills.
3. **Test skills.** You can test your students' technology skills by giving them multiple-choice and task-based exams. Following are examples from each type of test:
   - All of the following are reasons that writers should use their word processor's styles feature when creating technical documents EXCEPT
     - Styles save the writers' time.
     - Styles help ensure consistency.
     - Styles make collaboration easier.
     - Styles make it easier to print documents. (Correct)
   - Reformat the attached Word document in the following manner by using the Styles and Formatting task pane. If you do not have any of the typefaces listed below, choose another one.
     - Change the first heading to the predefined style called Heading 1.
     - Change all subheads to the predefined style called Heading 2.
     - For the list, apply the predefined style called 1. List Number 2.
     - For the second (not the first) paragraph of the document, create a new style called myindent with the following formatting features:
       - Based on predefined style body text first indent
       - Bookman typeface (any version)
4. **Incorporate technology requirements in major assignments.** Adding technology requirements to your major assignments helps emphasize the role of technology as a tool to achieve rhetorical goals. For example, for a report analyzing the effectiveness of a Web site, require students to use screen captures in their report or use data available in a PDF file.

A Final Word about Teaching Technology Skills

The focus of any tech-comm course is rhetoric. What we want our students to learn is how to create effective documents that respond to readers' needs. To accomplish this goal, students need to acquire and use technology skills. Although our focus should not be on training students how to use software, we should build into our courses opportunities for students to learn and practice basic technology skills that will help them write in the academic world and in the professional workplace.

Teaching Distance Education with *Technical Communication*

by John T. Battalio

Colleges and universities seeking to conserve campus resources and satisfy nontraditional students are turning increasingly to distance-education courses. Instructors who need to adapt their syllabi and other course materials for an online environment will find that Mike Markel's *Technical Communication* and its book companion site, TechComm Web <bedfordstmartins.com/techcomm>, provide many resources that can help make the distance-education course satisfying and productive for themselves and the students. In this article I discuss first some of the features of the text and the companion site that I use in my distance course, then I offer several strategies to help instructors manage their own distance courses. Finally, I offer a set of links that you might want to consult.

Useful Text and Web Site Features for Distance Education

Successful distance-ed students must be self-motivated people who can manage their time effectively and who are reasonably comfortable with computers. Perhaps most important, they must be able to learn independently. *Technical Communication* and TechComm Web provide students with numerous features that help ensure a successful online-learning experience. These features also benefit you as an instructor because they help the course flow more smoothly, lessen the amount of instructional materials you must prepare, and minimize students' questions. I have used *Technical Communication* in an Internet-based introductory technical communication course for the past four years and have found it a valuable resource. Here are eight features of the text and companion site that I use when teaching in an online environment.

1. **Sample documents in the text.** Distance-ed students need sample documents to help them apply the concepts they are studying to the documents they are producing. The many sample documents in the text are particularly effective because they relate to text discussions and include explanatory callouts that focus students' attention on the major parts of the sample documents.
2. **Interactive Sample Documents.** I use the Interactive Sample Documents in each chapter and on TechComm Web to generate online discussions of concepts in the text, helping students reinforce their understanding of key concepts.
3. **Guidelines Boxes.** I point students to the Guidelines Boxes to help them learn the important concepts in each chapter. Because the text provides this summary information for students specifically to help them prepare for quizzes and complete assignments, I get fewer student inquiries.
4. **Revision Checklists.** I encourage distance-ed students to use the Revision Checklists at the end of each chapter as reference material when they write their assignments and prepare for quizzes and tests.
5. **Flashcards on TechComm Web.** Because distance-ed students must learn on their own, they need more supplemental resources to assist them in completing the course successfully. I encourage them to use the flashcards to test their understanding of the key terms and concepts in each chapter.
6. **Forms for Technical Communication.** Among the forms provided in the textbook and on TechComm Web are two types of collaborative forms: a log for students to keep track of and evaluate their own progress, and a checklist to evaluate group

members. I find these forms essential in evaluating student performance because I do not have the opportunity to gauge the progress and cooperation of groups in class.

7. **Online Quizzes.** Distance-ed students have fewer opportunities for immediate feedback from their instructors; to help fill this gap, I use the Online Quizzes on TechComm Web as part of my course grading.
8. **Additional Exercises, Projects, and Cases.** I use the additional activities on Tech-Comm Web—each with suggested responses on the instructor site—to minimize the time I need to spend making up activities.
9. **Tutorials.** I always have my students read Mike Markel's tutorial "Designing for the Web" on TechComm Web. I will also require that they read the three new online tutorials provided on TechComm Web—"Evaluating Online Sources," "Preparing Presentation Slides," and "Designing Documents with a Word Processor." These tutorials guide students through some of their most common communication challenges.

Strategies for Developing Successful Distance-Ed Courses

Distance-ed instructors have four primary duties:

- Organize the course so that it meets the needs of online students.
- Tell students what they need to do and when.
- Provide general information and overviews of the topics and assignments.
- Provide forums for students to interact with both the instructor and their class-mates. These forums enable students to discuss the readings and assignments and to get feedback about their work in progress.

Consider these seven strategies to help you accomplish these goals.

1. **Send an e-mail to students a week before class begins.** In this introductory message, describe the prerequisites for the course, list the required software, describe your printing capability, explain how to access the course Web site, describe your expectations, and describe the qualities of a successful distance-ed student. This e-mail helps make the first week of class run smoothly and discourages students who aren't right for the online learning environment.
2. **Provide a weekly overview that students can easily scan.** On the first day of each week, provide a brief overview of that week's assignments. I use a template to keep the format of the overview standard from week to week so that students become familiar with it. The overview should have clear headings and no more than two or three screens of information. A typical format might begin with a bulleted list of the assignments and activities for the week, including due dates, followed by a summary of weekly point totals and the percentage of assignments completed, followed by brief explanations of the topics covered that week. Topic summaries should discuss briefly the highlights of the week's text reading, direct your students to the relevant parts of the textbook and Web site, and clearly state your expectations. If you assign weekly activities, like a short memo or document evaluation, it's best not to list the weekly assignments separately because some students might not read explanations accompanying the assignment. Rather, explanations of activities and assignments are best interwoven within content descriptions to help ensure that students understand the context of your assignments.
3. **Require draft submissions to a public forum before submitting major assignments.** For major assignments like proposals and reports, have students submit drafts of all or part of their assignments to a public forum like a discussion board,

where you might comment on their submissions. Your students will then be able to read each other's drafts as well as your own comments about their submissions. This process gives students access not only to many sample drafts but also to your reactions to these drafts. It is an excellent way to provide distance students with much-needed feedback. I receive more positive comments from students about these draft-submission activities than about any other activity.

4. **Assign weekly activities.** I use weekly activities not only to give students feedback but also to let me know which students are active participants and how well the class understands the course material. These activities should be simple assignments meant to give your students confidence that they understand the main concepts being covered. Consequently, they should focus on key information or become lead-ins for larger assignments. You can find excellent activities in the exercises following each textbook chapter or in the Additional Exercises, Projects, and Cases section of TechComm Web. These activities do not have to be a burden to grade. For instance, students might post their responses to a discussion board, where you and they react to these posts. You might also use these activities to initiate simple group assignments to help students learn how to manage group work online. Group work, of course, minimizes grading time.
5. **Require Reading Quizzes.** Just as in live classes, some distance-ed students will not read the assignments. Unlike live classes, however, these students will not have your lectures and class discussions to fill the void. Consequently, Reading Quizzes are an essential part of the online course. To encourage students to read assignments, I require that they submit responses to selected chapter quiz questions. Many students responding to my end-of-course evaluations say that, without these quizzes, they probably would not have completed all of the assigned readings.
6. **Promptly respond to student e-mail.** Because distance-ed students are eager for feedback, you should respond to their e-mail as soon as possible. Responding daily will save you time in the long run because you will be able to answer questions in a timely manner and satisfy the occasional student who will e-mail you continually until you respond. Here are three important tips to remember when responding to student e-mail:
   a. *If students ask you questions that you have already discussed in a weekly overview or that are explained in the textbook, send these students to the online materials or the textbook rather than answer their questions directly.* Some instructors think that responding fully to every e-mail makes the class more personal. But what will likely happen is that students will simply e-mail you whenever they have questions, rather than look for the answers themselves, thereby failing to take responsibility for their own learning and increasing your work load significantly.
   b. *When responding to student e-mail, copy yourself.* If the e-mail does not arrive or is inadvertently lost by the student, you can resend your copy without having to rewrite a response.
   c. *Include the student's name (or abbreviation) in the subject line of your e-mail messages.* The student's name helps you to locate specific e-mail messages more easily, particularly when sending messages to more than one student at once and when students' e-mail addresses as shown in the FROM line are not informative.
7. **Require collaborative forms for group work.** Because you do not have face-to-face contact with your collaborative groups, you will need feedback from collaborative forms. Here are two tips to increase your success in managing collaborative groups online:
   a. *Introduce the process by assigning two or three simple collaborative assignments, for instance, responding to a document or submitting a memo.* Your goal in this initial

collaborative effort should be to help students learn to communicate with each other online.

b. *Initially, you should assign students to groups, varying membership to help them get to know each other.* Then, for major assignments like proposals and reports, you might allow students to select their own partners.

Technical Communication and TechComm Web are valuable resources for teaching in an online environment. The many features that I use in traditional live courses also help distance-ed students learn in an online environment. Bottom line: I spend less time on repetitive chores, and that means more time to teach.

Links on Distance Education and Technical Communication

Mike Markel's article "Distance Education and the Myth of the New Pedagogy" was originally published in the *Journal of Business and Technical Communication* (February 13, 1999, pp. 208–22) and is now available from Ingenta <http://www.ingenta.com> free as a PDF file. (In Ingenta, search for *Distance Education and the Myth*.) In this article, Mike argues that the same teaching skills you use in the traditional classroom will serve you well in the distance classroom.

Barry Willis's set of guides, "Distance Education at a Glance" <www.uidaho.edu/eo/distglan.html> from Engineering Outreach at the University of Idaho, is a comprehensive set of brief discussions on the theory and practice of distance education.

Katy Campbell's "The Web: Design for Active Learning" <www.atl.ualberta.ca/articles/idesign/activel.cfm> from the University of Alberta's Academic Technologies for Learning, presents useful background on the principles of cognitive psychology that make for an effective distance-ed pedagogy.

"Interaction Options for Learning in the Virtual Classroom" <www.atl.ualberta.ca/articles/disted/interact_options.cfm> also from the University of Alberta's Academic Technologies for Learning, describes the technologies used for encouraging interaction in distance courses.

"Distance Education for Technical Writing" <www.uwm.edu/People/alred/litreview-model.pdf>, an anonymous student's literature review of technical communication and distance education, contains a useful bibliography.

2. Major Features of *Technical Communication* and TechComm Web

Technical Communication and its companion site, TechComm Web <bedfordstmartins.com/techcomm>, are a practical, comprehensive, and fully integrated pair of tools for college and university tech-comm courses. They can be used effectively by all teachers, from those who have no practical experience as technical writers and have never taught the course before, to experienced tech-comm instructors with substantial tech-comm experience.

In writing the book and designing the Web site, I focused on three key ideas:

- *Students should study real technical communication.* All the examples in the text, from individual sentences to completion reports, are real, having been written by professionals in business, industry, or government, or by students while they were employed in the outside world. TechComm Web extends the text by directing students to the numerous resources and examples of technical communication available on the World Wide Web.
- *Students should start with the principles of technical communication before studying the more sophisticated applications.* The text begins with chapters that help students understand the context in which tech comm is produced. Then it presents process-based instruction to help students plan, draft, and revise the textual and visual elements of their documents. Finally, the text discusses the various applications, from correspondence to job-application materials, proposals, reports, instructions, Web sites, and oral presentations.
- *Students should do a lot of analysis, evaluation, and revision.* The text contains a wealth of evaluation and revision exercises based on both professional and student writing. These exercises will be of great value to instructors who do not have their own tech-comm samples for students to study. In addition, these exercises help all instructors make the point that in the outside world many, if not most, writing assignments are collaborative. This text will give students a real sense of editing someone else's draft. Part 4 of this *Instructor's Resource Manual* includes guidelines for all the exercises, projects, and cases presented in the text. TechComm Web provides numerous additional activities; suggested responses for all of these activities are provided in the Instructor Resources section on the site. Every month TechComm Web introduces new teaching materials.

Technical Communication

Technical Communication consists of five parts:

- Part One, "The Technical Communication Environment," introduces tech comm and discusses ethical and legal issues students need to understand. It also includes a chapter on the writing process as it is applied in technical communication, as well as a chapter on collaborative writing. Part One provides the background that students need to understand the distinctive characteristics of the writing process in technical communication.
- Part Two, "Planning the Document," includes chapters on analyzing audience and purpose, on persuasion, on primary and secondary research techniques, and on organizing information.

- Part Three, "Developing the Textual Elements," discusses how to draft and revise the textual elements that appear in documents. This part includes chapters on writing definitions and descriptions, on improving textual coherence, on improving sentences, and on preparing front and back matter.
- Part Four, "Developing the Visual Elements," includes chapters on designing the document and the page and on creating graphics.
- Part Five, "Applications," contains chapters focusing on common applications: letters, memos, and e-mails; job-application materials; proposals; informal reports; formal reports; instructions and manuals; Web sites; and oral presentations. In this part, one report topic (on a feasibility study for buying new printers) is addressed in a proposal, a progress report, a completion report, and an oral presentation.

Each chapter of *Technical Communication* includes a number of features that reinforce the concepts and skills described in the chapter:

- *Interactive Sample Document:* an example of real tech comm, accompanied by questions that require students to apply the concepts they have studied in the chapter. Answers to the questions are provided in Part 4 of this manual and on TechComm Web. TechComm Web also provides additional Interactive Sample Documents with responses for Chapters 15–22.
- *Strategies for Intercultural Communication:* brief discussions of how to confront the challenges of communicating with people from other cultures.
- *Revision checklist:* a tool that helps students remember key points as they plan, draft, and revise their documents.
- *Exercises:* assignments that can be carried out in 15 minutes in networked or nonnetworked classrooms.
- *Projects:* more complex assignments that can be completed by students working alone or collaboratively.
- *Cases:* realistic scenarios in which students try to determine how to confront a communication challenge.

An easy and effective way to determine whether the students have read and understood the assigned material is to use the exercises, projects, and cases as diagnostic tests, either as out-of-class assignments or as material for in-class discussions. Alternatively, you can have students make oral presentations. The revision exercises, because they are real examples of technical communication, yield no simple solutions. When you get to the various end-of-chapter activities, you will see that while most instructors would agree with the diagnosis of the problem in a particular one, many different strategies could be used in revising the samples. This, I think, is as it should be. Students are used to thinking in terms of "correct" answers, especially in English class. Open-ended exercises help them see that there are a number of different approaches to any writing exercise and that the writer must be able to justify the revision articulately. The burden of choice falls squarely on the student's shoulders, as it will on the job.

TechComm Web

TechComm Web is another valuable teaching resource. It is divided into two main sections: one for instructors and one for students. The Instructor Resources section has eight major features:

1. **Teaching Topics.** Downloadable versions of the four Teaching Topics: "Making the Transition from Comp to Tech Comm," "Addressing Plagiarism in the Tech-Comm Course," "Integrating Technology in the Tech-Comm Course," and "Teaching Distance Education with *Technical Communication.*"
2. **Sample Syllabi.** Downloadable versions of the five schedules found in this manual, a link to Mike Markel's full syllabus for the service course in technical communication, and links to syllabi from sixth edition users.
3. **Chapter Summaries.** Electronic versions of the same chapter summaries that appear in this manual.
4. **PowerPoint Slides.** PowerPoint slides of the main bullet lists in the book are easy to modify for your own in-class use.
5. **Transparency Masters.** Transparency masters of most of the figures and tables in the book.
6. **Reading Quizzes.** A set of reading quizzes that can be downloaded and modified for use in class. These quizzes call for more expansive answers than the Online Quizzes.
7. **Suggested Responses.** Responses for all of the exercises, projects, and cases in the book, as well as for the additional exercises, projects, and cases in the Student Resources section on TechComm Web. Answers to questions contained in the tutorials can also be found here.
8. **Quiz Tracking.** Access to your students' results on the Online Quizzes.

The Student Resources section has seven major features:

1. **Links Library.** This section includes links to all the sites listed in the marginal annotations in the book, as well as to the sites shown in the screen captures. In addition, this section includes links to other Web sites showing the principles and applications discussed in the chapter.
2. **Interactive Sample Documents.** Online versions of each of the Interactive Sample Documents in the book, plus eight additional Interactive Sample Documents for Chapters 15–22, all with suggested answers to the questions.
3. **Tutorials.** Four tutorials help students understand and apply important concepts in tech comm. Each tutorial includes an overview of principles and abundant samples for evaluation. Topics include evaluating online sources, designing documents with a word processor, preparing presentation slides, and designing Web sites.
4. **Online Quizzes.** These 10-question multiple-choice quizzes yield immediate grades and feedback on students' understanding of the chapter, directing them to the page in *Technical Communication* on which the topic is discussed. Instructors can use the Quiz Tracking feature to record their students' grades on the Online Quizzes.
5. **Flashcards.** Covering vocabulary and concepts explained in each chapter, online flashcards help students reinforce their understanding of terms used in the text.
6. **Additional Exercises, Projects, and Cases.** Students have access to these additional activities not included in the book. Suggested responses are available in the Instructor Resources section on the site.
7. **Forms for Technical Communication.** These student forms from the book can be downloaded for use in collaborative writing, in analyzing audience, and in evaluating oral presentations.

3. Sample Syllabus and Schedules

Technical Communication and TechComm Web provide a great deal of information, more than an instructor could cover in one semester. In this section I present five sample schedules that offer a range of options for teaching different sorts of courses to students with various needs and interests. Of course, you can modify these schedules to meet your own preferences and varying semester lengths.

Each schedule presents the chapters in the sequence in which they appear in the text. However, you might want to change the sequence. For instance, some instructors like to begin the semester with an application such as the job-application materials that gets the students writing and introduces principles such as audience analysis, page design, and letter writing. Other instructors like to start with sentence-level rhetoric. The marginal cross-references in the text make it easy for you and your students to find information on related topics in other chapters and on TechComm Web. Another way in which you might want to modify the sample schedules is to include classroom time for quizzes, tests, in-class writing, collaborative group work, or online activities.

These schedules show basic discussion topics and suggested weekly writing assignments and online activities from which to choose. The nature of your course and your students will determine the best way to use your class time. Consult the chapter-by-chapter guide in Part 4 of this *Instructor's Resource Manual* for specific suggestions on how to teach the different topics.

My current syllabus, complete with detailed descriptions of the writing assignments, is available on TechComm Web <bedfordstmartins.com/techcomm>. Help yourself to anything you like.

The five sample schedules presented in this section are

- a one-semester survey course focusing on rhetoric and basic applications
- a one-semester survey course focusing on rhetoric and advanced applications
- a first-semester course for tech-comm majors
- a second-semester course for tech-comm majors
- a one-quarter survey course focusing on rhetoric and basic applications

Schedule: One-Semester Survey Course on Rhetoric and Basic Applications

This schedule is made for courses that focus on an introduction to tech comm and its most common applications. It emphasizes the rhetoric of tech comm—the material from the first four parts of the text. It would be most appropriate for courses at many junior colleges and community colleges and for sophomore-level courses at many colleges and universities.

Week One

First hour: Introduction to course
Second hour: Chapter 1. Introduction to Technical Communication
Third hour: Chapter 2. Understanding Ethical and Legal Considerations
ASSIGNMENT: Chapter 1, Project 2

Week Two

First two hours: Chapter 3. Understanding the Writing Process
Third hour: Chapter 4. Writing Collaboratively
ASSIGNMENT: Chapter 3, Case: The Writing Process Online

Week Three

First hour: Chapter 4. Writing Collaboratively
Second and third hours: Chapter 5. Analyzing Your Audience and Purpose
ASSIGNMENT: Chapter 5, Project 3

Week Four

First and second hours: Chapter 6. Communicating Persuasively
Third hour: Chapter 7. Researching Your Subject; Tutorial "Evaluating Online Sources"
ASSIGNMENT: Chapter 7, Exercise 2

Week Five

First and second hours: Chapter 7. Researching Your Subject
Third hour: Chapter 8. Organizing Your Information
ASSIGNMENT: Chapter 8, Exercise 3

Week Six

First hour: Chapter 8. Organizing Your Information
Second and third hours: Chapter 9. Drafting and Revising Definitions and Descriptions
ASSIGNMENT: Chapter 9, Project 5

Week Seven

First hour: Chapter 9. Drafting and Revising Definitions and Descriptions
Second and third hours: Chapter 10. Drafting and Revising Coherent Documents
ASSIGNMENT: Chapter 9, Project 7

Week Eight

First hour: Chapter 10. Drafting and Revising Coherent Documents
Second and third hours: Chapter 11. Drafting and Revising Effective Sentences
ASSIGNMENT: Chapter 10, Exercises 3 and 4

Week Nine

First and second hours: Chapter 12. Drafting and Revising Front and Back Matter
Third hour: Chapter 13. Designing the Document; Tutorial "Designing Documents with a Word Processor"
ASSIGNMENT: Chapter 12, Case: Planning for Better Front and Back Matter

Week Ten

First hour: Chapter 13. Designing the Document
Second and third hours: Chapter 14. Creating Graphics
ASSIGNMENT: Chapter 13, Project 3

Week Eleven

First hour: Chapter 14. Creating Graphics
Second and third hours: Chapter 15. Writing Letters, Memos, and E-mails
ASSIGNMENT: Chapter 14, Exercise 4

Week Twelve

First hour: Chapter 15. Writing Letters, Memos, and E-mails
Second and third hours: Chapter 16. Preparing Job-Application Materials
ASSIGNMENT: Chapter 16, Project 6

Week Thirteen

All three hours: Chapter 18. Writing Informal Reports
ASSIGNMENT: Chapter 18, Case: Amending a Proposal

Week Fourteen

First and second hours: Chapter 20. Writing Instructions and Manuals
Third hour: Chapter 22. Making Oral Presentations; Tutorial "Preparing Presentation Slides"
ASSIGNMENT: Chapter 20, Exercise 2

Week Fifteen

All three hours: Delivery of oral presentations (Chapter 22, Project 3)

Schedule: One-Semester Survey Course on Rhetoric and Advanced Applications

This schedule is made for courses that introduce tech comm and its more-advanced applications, such as proposals, completion reports, and oral presentations. This approach would be useful for courses taken by upperclass students at many colleges and universities.

Week One

First hour: Introduction to course
Second hour: Chapter 1. Introduction to Technical Communication
Third hour: Chapter 2. Understanding Ethical and Legal Considerations
ASSIGNMENT: Chapter 1, Project 2

Week Two

First two hours: Chapter 3. Understanding the Writing Process
Third hour: Chapter 4. Writing Collaboratively
ASSIGNMENT: Chapter 3, Case: The Writing Process Online

Week Three

First hour: Chapter 4. Writing Collaboratively
Second hour: Chapter 5. Analyzing Your Audience and Purpose
Third hour: Chapter 6. Communicating Persuasively
ASSIGNMENT: Chapter 5, Project 3

Week Four

First hour: Chapter 6. Communicating Persuasively
Second and third hours: Chapter 7. Researching Your Subject; Tutorial "Evaluating Online Sources"
ASSIGNMENT: Chapter 7, Exercise 2

Week Five

First hour: Chapter 7. Researching Your Subject
Second and third hours: Chapter 8. Organizing Your Information
ASSIGNMENT: Chapter 8, Exercise 3

Week Six

First and second hours: Chapter 9. Drafting and Revising Definitions and Descriptions
Third hour: Chapter 10. Drafting and Revising Coherent Documents
ASSIGNMENT: Chapter 9, Project 5

Week Seven

First and second hours: Chapter 10. Drafting and Revising Coherent Documents
Third hour: Chapter 11. Drafting and Revising Effective Sentences
ASSIGNMENT: Chapter 10, Exercises 3, 4, 5, and 6

Week Eight

First hour: Chapter 11. Drafting and Revising Effective Sentences
Second and third hours: Chapter 12. Drafting and Revising Front and Back Matter
ASSIGNMENT: Chapter 12, Case: Planning for Better Front and Back Matter

Week Nine

First and second hours: Chapter 13. Designing the Document; Tutorial "Designing Documents with a Word Processor"
Third hour: Chapter 14. Creating Graphics
ASSIGNMENT: Chapter 13, Case: The Underdesigned Data Sheet

Week Ten

First hour: Chapter 14. Creating Graphics
Second and third hours: Chapter 15. Writing Letters, Memos, and E-mails
ASSIGNMENT: Chapter 14, Exercise 4

Week Eleven

First and second hours: Chapter 16. Preparing Job-Application Materials
Third hour: Chapter 17. Writing Proposals
ASSIGNMENT: Chapter 16, Project 6

Week Twelve

First hour: Chapter 17. Writing Proposals
Second and third hours: Chapter 18. Writing Informal Reports
ASSIGNMENT: Chapter 17, Project 3

Week Thirteen

First two hours: Chapter 19. Writing Formal Reports
Third hour: Chapter 20. Writing Instructions and Manuals
ASSIGNMENT: Chapter 19, Project 3

Week Fourteen

First hour: Chapter 20. Writing Instructions and Manuals
Second hour: Chapter 22. Making Oral Presentations; Tutorial "Preparing Presentation Slides"
ASSIGNMENT: Chapter 20, Project 4

Week Fifteen

First two hours: Delivery of oral presentations (Chapter 22, Project 3)
Third hour: Workshop on completion reports

Schedule: First-Semester Course for Tech-Comm Majors

This schedule is made for the first course of a two-semester sequence for tech-comm majors and other students spending two semesters on tech comm. This syllabus concentrates on the rhetoric of tech comm. (The second-semester course focuses on the applications.)

Week One

First hour: Introduction to course
Second hour: Chapter 1. Introduction to Technical Communication
Third hour: Chapter 2. Understanding Ethical and Legal Considerations
ASSIGNMENT: Chapter 1, Case: Practicing What We Preach

Week Two

First two hours: Chapter 2. Understanding Ethical and Legal Considerations
Third hour: Chapter 3. Understanding the Writing Process
ASSIGNMENT: Chapter 2, Case: The Name Game

Week Three

First hour: Chapter 3. Understanding the Writing Process
Second and third hours: Chapter 4. Writing Collaboratively
ASSIGNMENT: Chapter 3, Case: The Writing Process Online

Week Four

First hour: Chapter 4. Writing Collaboratively
Second and third hours: Chapter 5. Analyzing Your Audience and Purpose
ASSIGNMENT: Chapter 4, Case: The Reluctant Collaborator

Week Five

All three hours: Chapter 6. Communicating Persuasively
ASSIGNMENT: Chapter 6, Case: Being Persuasive about Privacy

Week Six

All three hours: Chapter 7. Researching Your Subject; Tutorial "Evaluating Online Sources"
ASSIGNMENT: Chapter 7, Project 6

Week Seven

All three hours: Chapter 8. Organizing Your Information
ASSIGNMENT: Chapter 8, Case: Introducing a Document

Week Eight

All three hours: Chapter 9. Drafting and Revising Definitions and Descriptions
ASSIGNMENT: Chapter 9, Case: Describing a New Fighter Jet

Week Nine

All three hours: Chapter 10. Drafting and Revising Coherent Documents
ASSIGNMENT: Chapter 10, Case: Writing Guidelines about Coherence

Week Ten

All three hours: Chapter 11. Drafting and Revising Effective Sentences
ASSIGNMENT: Chapter 11, Exercises 1–25

Week Eleven

All three hours: Chapter 12. Drafting and Revising Front and Back Matter
ASSIGNMENT: Chapter 12, Case: Planning for Better Front and Back Matter

Week Twelve

All three hours: Chapter 13. Designing the Document; Tutorial "Designing Documents with a Word Processor"
ASSIGNMENT: Chapter 13, Case: The Underdesigned Data Sheet

Week Thirteen

All three hours: Chapter 14. Creating Graphics
ASSIGNMENT: Chapter 14, Exercise 4

Week Fourteen

All three hours: Chapter 15. Writing Letters, Memos, and E-mails
ASSIGNMENT: Chapter 15, Project 8

Week Fifteen

All three hours: Chapter 16. Preparing Job-Application Materials
ASSIGNMENT: Chapter 16, Project 6

Schedule: Second-Semester Course for Tech-Comm Majors

This schedule is made for the second course of a two-semester sequence for tech-comm majors and other students spending two semesters on tech comm. This syllabus concentrates on the major applications of tech comm.

Week One

All three hours: Chapter 17. Writing Proposals

Week Two

All three hours: Chapter 17. Writing Proposals
ASSIGNMENT: Chapter 17, Project 3

Week Three

All three hours: Chapter 18. Writing Informal Reports
ASSIGNMENT: Chapter 18, Project 4

Week Four

All three hours: Workshops on proposals

Week Five
All three hours: Workshops on informal reports

Week Six
All three hours: Chapter 19. Writing Formal Reports

Week Seven
All three hours: Chapter 19. Writing Formal Reports
ASSIGNMENT: Chapter 19, Project 3

Week Eight
All three hours: Chapter 20. Writing Instructions and Manuals

Week Nine
All three hours: Chapter 20. Writing Instructions and Manuals
ASSIGNMENT: Chapter 20, Project 4

Week Ten
All three hours: Chapter 21. Creating Web Sites
ASSIGNMENT: Chapter 21, Case: Creating a Web Site

Week Eleven
All three hours: Workshop on instructions and manuals

Week Twelve
All three hours: Tutorial "Designing for the Web"

Week Thirteen
All three hours: Chapter 22. Making Oral Presentations, Tutorial "Preparing Presentation Slides"
ASSIGNMENT: Chapter 22, Project 4

Week Fourteen
All three hours: Workshop on Web sites

Week Fifteen
All three hours: Delivery of oral presentations (Chapter 22, Project 4)

Schedule: One-Quarter Survey Course on Rhetoric and Basic Applications

This schedule is made for 10-week courses that focus on an introduction to tech comm and its most common applications. This syllabus emphasizes the rhetoric of tech comm—the material from the first four parts of the text. It would be most appropriate for courses at many junior colleges and community colleges and for sophomore-level courses at many colleges and universities.

Week One

First hour: Introduction to course
Second hour: Chapter 1. Introduction to Technical Communication
Third hour: Chapter 2. Understanding Ethical and Legal Considerations
ASSIGNMENT: Chapter 1, Project 2

Week Two

First two hours: Chapter 3. Understanding the Writing Process
Third hour: Chapter 5. Analyzing Your Audience and Purpose
ASSIGNMENT: Chapter 3, Case: The Writing Process Online

Week Three

First and second hours: Chapter 5. Analyzing Your Audience and Purpose
Third hour: Chapter 6. Communicating Persuasively
ASSIGNMENT: Chapter 5, Project 3

Week Four

First hour: Chapter 6. Communicating Persuasively
Second and third hours: Chapter 7. Researching Your Subject; Tutorial "Evaluating Online Sources"
ASSIGNMENT: Chapter 7, Exercise 2

Week Five

First and second hours: Chapter 8. Organizing Your Information
Third hour: Chapter 9. Drafting and Revising Definitions and Descriptions
ASSIGNMENT: Chapter 8, Exercise 3

Week Six

First hour: Chapter 9. Drafting and Revising Definitions and Descriptions
Second and third hours: Chapter 10. Drafting and Revising Coherent Documents
ASSIGNMENT: Chapter 9, Project 5

Week Seven

First and second hours: Chapter 11. Drafting and Revising Effective Sentences
Third hour: Chapter 13. Designing the Document; Tutorial "Designing Documents with a Word Processor"
ASSIGNMENT: Chapter 13, Project 3

Week Eight

First hour: Chapter 13. Designing the Document
Second and third hours: Chapter 14. Creating Graphics
ASSIGNMENT: Chapter 14, Exercise 4

Week Nine

First and second hours: Chapter 15. Writing Letters, Memos, and E-mails
Third hour: Chapter 18. Writing Informal Reports
ASSIGNMENT: Chapter 15, Project 8

Week Ten

First hour: Chapter 18. Writing Informal Reports
Second and third hours: Chapter 20. Writing Instructions and Manuals
ASSIGNMENT: Chapter 20, Exercise 2

4. Chapter-by-Chapter Guide to *Technical Communication*

This part of the *Instructor's Resource Manual* provides advice on how to get the most out of each of the 22 chapters of *Technical Communication* and the accompanying resources on TechComm Web <bedfordstmartins.com/techcomm>. The discussion of each chapter consists of five parts:

1. **A summary of the content of the chapter.** This summary helps you quickly review what your students have read.
2. **A list of teaching goals for the chapter.** Do not feel that you have to accomplish every goal listed. You will likely find yourself spending less time on some chapters and more time—sometimes several class meetings—on those that help your students meet the overall goals for your course.
3. **Teaching guide for a typical class meeting.** This section contains brief commentary on teaching chapter concepts as well as teaching approaches for both *traditional* classrooms and *technology-enhanced* classrooms.
   a. *Teaching approaches for traditional classrooms.* These activities can be adapted to most traditional-classroom environments. In some cases, you will need to plan ahead and prepare handouts or transparencies of information available on TechComm Web or elsewhere online.
   b. *Teaching approaches for technology-enhanced classrooms.* Although your resources will vary, I define technology-enhanced classrooms as having at least computers with Internet access for most of the students and a video/data LCD projector for you to use. I also assume each computer has standard Microsoft Office applications (Word, Excel, and PowerPoint). Depending on your technology resources, discussions can take place face-to-face, asynchronously over e-mail and discussion boards, or synchronously in online forums.

   I list more activities than you can comfortably cover in a single 55–75-minute class meeting. Moreover, you will need to budget time for classroom-management activities (for example, taking roll, returning assignments, and so on) and other important class activities such as explaining assignments, peer-review workshops, and quizzes. Consequently, consider the approaches as a menu of class activities and discussion topics from which to build your lesson plans.

   The times listed for each activity are estimates. The amount of time you need to budget will vary depending on the number of students in your class, the depth of discussion you seek, and the scope of your course. Many of the activities I list are described in greater detail in the additional exercises, projects, and cases provided in the Student Resources section of TechComm Web. Because new class activities are periodically added to the site, I recommend you check the site every so often during the semester.
4. **Suggestions for responding to the Interactive Sample Documents in the book.** I provide brief answers to the questions that accompany the Interactive Sample Document in each chapter. You can find these responses and additional Interactive Sample Documents for chapters 15–22 on TechComm Web.
5. **Suggested responses to the exercises, projects, and cases in the book.** You will find exercises, projects, and cases at the end of each chapter in *Technical Communication*. Additional exercises, projects, and cases are included in the Student Resources section of TechComm Web, and responses for those additional activities, as well as the responses found in this manual, are included in the Instructor Resources section

of TechComm Web. Whenever possible, I provide answers to the exercises with a single solution. In many of the assignments, your students' responses will vary considerably. For these I provide brief commentary on what to look for in a successful response or the reason that you might want to assign the exercise, project, or case.

PART ONE: THE TECHNICAL COMMUNICATION ENVIRONMENT

Chapter 1. Introduction to Technical Communication

A. Summary

Technical communication is the process of creating, shaping, and communicating technical information so that people can use it safely, effectively, and efficiently. It is created by technical professionals (engineers, scientists, businesspeople) and by technical communicators (full-time writers, editors, document-production people). Tech comm is essential in business and industry because virtually every action taken has to be communicated to subordinates or supervisors, or both, and has to be documented to provide a record for future reference. Technical documents are addressed to particular readers, help those readers solve problems, are part of an organizational context, are often created collaboratively, use design to increase readability, involve graphics, and involve high-tech tools. Effective tech comm is honest, clear, accurate, comprehensive, accessible, concise, professional in appearance, and correct.

B. Goals

By the end of the chapter, students should be able to do the following:

1. define technical communication and its role in their careers
2. distinguish between the two categories of people who produce technical communication
3. list examples of technical communication in business and industry
4. describe the seven major characteristics of technical communication
5. explain the eight measures of excellence in technical communication

C. Teaching Guide

Technical communication is usually described in one of two ways. Some people hold that technical communication is nonfiction writing about science, engineering, or technology. Others (including myself) place no such subject-area boundaries on the description. In teaching heterogeneous students, I find the more inclusive description preferable because it does not exclude any students, such as design or journalism majors. Another reason I prefer the second description is that the first description can create a male bias, which is not only unfair but also inaccurate.

Students in tech-comm courses generally need little motivation. Most of them have learned from job interviews (or from friends who have been on interviews) that effective communication skills are not simply an asset but a necessity. If your students are less advanced, you might refer to the sample classified ad in Chapter 1, which mentions communication skills explicitly as one of the requirements.

Of the eight measures of excellence of technical communication, three might require some comment in class. Accessibility, the ease with which the different readers can locate the information they seek, is a new concept to many students. Even though they might be experienced in using headings in lab reports, they often think that a technical document, like a paper in freshman English, ought to consist of long paragraphs marching proudly down the page. The concept of lists is alien to most students.

Conciseness is another difficult concept for most students. The academic world deals almost exclusively in minimum-length requirements. Rarely does a student hear that an assignment must be less than 10 pages.

Correctness is a concept the students have heard, but in tech comm the explanation should be a little different from that in freshman comp. Writing should be correct primarily because readers will draw inferences about the quality of the technical information based on the correctness of the writing, even though a poor writer can be very intelligent.

Traditional-Classroom Approaches

1. Additional Exercise: The Syllabus as Technical Communication (see TechComm Web) asks students to examine your syllabus as a technical document. (15 minutes)
2. Additional Exercise: Addressing an Audience in a Web Site asks students to consider the importance of audience in technical communication. You will need substitute sample print documents aimed at different audiences and for different purposes for the Web sites mentioned. (15 minutes)
3. Additional Exercise: Evaluating the Accessibility of a Phone Book asks small groups of students to analyze phone books from the standpoint of accessibility. (15 minutes)
4. Bring in a collection of documents from your office and home. Be sure you include obvious technical documents that may or may not be considered technical communication, such as owner's manuals, letters, warranties, reports, memos, and schedules. Also, include other documents, such as recipes, poems, short stories, flyers, magazine articles, and sweepstakes offers. In small groups, have students use the seven characteristics of technical communication to decide which documents represent typical technical communication. You can also have the students speculate which category of people (technical professionals or technical communicators) produced the sample documents. Have the groups report their findings to the larger group. (20 minutes)
5. Using the technical documents you identified in item 4, have the groups choose one document to evaluate using the measures of excellence discussed in Chapter 1. Have them report their findings orally, or introduce memos and have them present their results in a memo. (20 minutes)

Technology-Enhanced Approaches

1. Additional Exercise: The Syllabus as Technical Communication asks students to examine your online syllabus as a technical document. As part of this activity, have students list the differences they note between your electronic syllabus and traditional paper syllabi with which they are familiar. Part of your discussion can focus on the differences between print and online documents. (15 minutes)
2. Additional Exercise: Evaluating Measures of Excellence in a Letter asks students to consider the importance of audience in technical communication. (15 minutes)
3. Additional Exercise: Learning about the Lives of Technical Communicators provides students with a glimpse of a technical communicator's work week. Ask students to record what they found surprising as well as their thoughts on how a technical communicator's week is different from a technical professional's week. As part of your discussion, you can highlight the role of interpersonal skills in all jobs. (20 minutes)
4. Supply students with a list of links to documents (some obviously technical and some not so clear-cut) on the Web. In small groups, have students use the seven characteristics of technical communication to decide which documents represent

typical technical communication. You can also have the students speculate which category of people (technical professionals or technical communicators) produced the sample documents. Have the groups report their findings to the larger group. (20 minutes)

5. Ask students to select one document from the list you supplied and have them evaluate it using the measures of excellence discussed in the chapter. (20 minutes)

D. Suggestions for Responding to the Interactive Sample Document

1. How have the writers used graphical elements in the sentence below the title to emphasize the message in that sentence?

The writers have used a different color (blue), a larger typeface, and italics to emphasize the phrase "get your job done."

2. In what other ways have the writers used words and graphics to make the document more interesting and appealing to readers?

Blue is used again in the diagrams that list the jobs—copy, print, scan, and fax—reinforcing the idea introduced in the blue text in the sentence above.

3. How have the writers used text and graphics to present the tasks that people can accomplish with this machine?

The photograph of the copier, with the callouts, starts to teach readers how to use the machine. Note that the callouts describe tasks—such as "turn the machine on/off here"—rather than features.

E. Suggestions for Responding to the Exercises, Projects, and Cases in the Book

These assignments ask students to put their responses in a memo. Since this chapter is often the first chapter covered in a course, many students will benefit from a brief discussion of how to format and organize a memo (see Chapter 15, page 378).

Exercise 1. Canon's Web page demonstrates most of the characteristics of technical communication. It addresses particular readers (those visitors to the site who are interested in Canon's products), reflects Canon's goals and culture, was produced collaboratively using high-tech tools, and consists of words and graphics. However, design flaws undercut its effectiveness. First, the descriptions of the three products pictured on the left are inconsistent: twice the description comes after the picture and once it comes before it. In addition, the graphic of the copy machine on the far right has its description below it in a different typeface. This site could be improved if the descriptions of the graphics were consistently formatted and placed.

You might also want to discuss with your students the extent to which this Web page demonstrates the measures of excellence of technical communication. Finally, you might discuss how it is possible to analyze the design of a document without necessarily understanding its content.

Project 2. Describing and evaluating a common technical document using the chapter's measures of excellence helps students notice the technical communication around them and learn the characteristics of excellent technical communication. Although responses will vary, successful responses will evaluate the owner's manual using the eight measures of excellence described in the chapter: honesty, clarity, accuracy, comprehensiveness, accessibility, conciseness, professional appearance, and correctness. In addition, successful responses will feature multiple examples from the sample manual to support and illustrate the evaluation.

Project 3. This project requires students to understand the definition of technical communication and to recognize its major characteristics. Although responses will vary, successful responses will identify a suitable technical document on the Web and use the characteristics and vocabulary from the chapter to describe it. Also, the evaluation of the document's effectiveness should be based on the measures of excellence described in the chapter.

Case: Practicing What We Preach
This case requires that students review the section in Chapter 1 called "Measures of Excellence in Technical Communication" and begin to think about how Web design differs from print design. Although responses will vary, successful ones will focus on the clarity of the site (how easy it is to understand the information in the site), comprehensiveness (how much information is contained in the site), accessibility (how easy it is to navigate the site), and professional appearance (how well the site presents a professional image for the chapter).

Chapter 2. Understanding Ethical and Legal Considerations

A. Summary

Many ethicists approach ethical dilemmas using four standards: rights (concerning the basic needs and welfare of particular individuals), justice (concerning how the positive and negative effects of an action or policy should be distributed fairly among a group), utility (concerning the positive and negative effects of an action or policy on the general public), and care (concerning our responsibilities to people in our family, workplace, and community).

Technical communicators should know the basics of four areas of law: copyright, trademark, contract, and liability. Copyright law, which covers the protection of the rights of the author, is often deliberately vague. Trademarks are different from registered trademarks, which provide substantial federal protection. Expressing trademarks correctly in communications can help protect them.

Companies are responsible for abiding by their express (explicit) warranties and implied warranties. And companies can reduce the incidence of injuries that can lead to liability claims by understanding the users of the product, writing safety messages that follow the principles of effective tech comm, and testing the instructions effectively and often.

Employees should be aware of their right to resist an employer's request or demand that they participate in an unethical action or that they look the other way while others participate. If the employee has exhausted all efforts to prevent or solve the unethical practice, he or she is entitled to blow the whistle. Technical communicators and technical professionals should abide by relevant laws and appropriate corporate and professional codes of conduct, tell the truth, avoid misleading readers, be clear, avoid discriminatory language, and acknowledge assistance from others.

B. Goals

By the end of the chapter, students should be able to do the following:

1. explain why technical communicators and technical professionals need to understand basic ethical and legal principles
2. understand the basics of four different bodies of law relevant to technical communication: copyright law, trademark law, contract law, and liability law
3. analyze a code of conduct

4. define whistleblowing
5. list the seven principles of ethical communication and use these principles to meet workplace obligations

C. Teaching Guide

In one sense, it is very difficult to talk about the ethics of tech comm because the subject is subtle and complicated, and there are no easy answers. However, most students have experienced serious ethical dilemmas at school or at work, and they are generally interested in talking about the subject.

Sometimes students want you to tell them what they should do when they confront ethical dilemmas, but of course you cannot. Sometimes students think that reading a chapter on ethics will make them ethical people. One of your jobs is to help them understand that they cannot "learn" how to be ethical; the purpose of the chapter is to help them understand how ethicists frame the issues, so that they can think about their own ethical dilemmas more clearly and sensitively.

Discussions of legal considerations are similarly challenging because students do not necessarily see themselves as being representatives of their organizations. But you have to help them see that when they communicate they represent the ethical stance of their organizations, and that this ethical stance is often a matter of legal concern. Try to help them see that the law is our society's principal means of manifesting its deepest ethical beliefs. Often there are liability cases in the news that can help you focus their attention on the relationship between ethics and the law.

Traditional-Classroom Approaches

1. Additional Exercise: Evaluating the American Chemical Society Code of Conduct (see TechComm Web) asks students to study the American Chemical Society's code of conduct. Have your students compare this code to the STC ethical guidelines. You will need to bring print copies of the ACS code to class. (15 minutes)
2. Help students learn the basics of copyright law, trademark law, contract law, and liability law by discussing current cases relating to these laws. You can find current cases by searching the Internet. Because these laws can be complicated, your goal should not be to give legal advice but to help students understand how each law focuses on different obligations a technical communicator has when writing technical documents. (15 minutes)
3. Discuss the concept of *whistleblowing*. Develop your own whistleblowing case or visit WorldWideWhistleblowers.com <www.worldwidewhistleblowers.com> and find a case applicable to technical communication. Click on Case Studies or News. Prepare a handout or describe the case orally and then have students answer the following questions:
   a. "Where does loyalty to the employer end and the employee's right to blow the whistle begin?"
   b. "What should an employee do before blowing the whistle?"
   c. "What is the difference between being *justified* in blowing the whistle and being *obligated* to do so?"
   d. "In what ways does doing the ethical thing help or hinder an employee's career?" (25 minutes)

Technology-Enhanced Approaches

1. Additional Exercise: Finding a Code of Conduct on a Web Site asks students to search for a code of conduct on the Web site of a large or important company related to their major. (20 minutes)

2. Additional Exercise: Evaluating the Institute of Scientific and Technical Communicators Code of Conduct asks students to take a closer look at the code of conduct of the Institute of Scientific and Technical Communicators. (20 minutes)
3. Additional Project: Analyzing an Engineering Ethics Case emphasizes the importance of clear, honest communication by having students examine ethics cases from engineering. (20 minutes)
4. Have students find information about a recent case of whistleblowing using Internet search engines. In a memo to you, have students summarize the case, describe its relevance to technical communication, and respond to the questions in item 3 under traditional-classroom approaches. (25 minutes)

D. Suggestions for Responding to the Interactive Sample Document

1. How effectively does this code protect the interests of the public rather than those of STC members? What specific words or phrases demonstrate this?

Much of this code effectively addresses ways that STC members strive to protect the interests of the public. The section on legality, for instance, focuses on adhering to laws and regulations and to abiding by contracts. The section on honesty states that STC members seek to promote the public good. Each of the sections of the code, in fact, includes language about protecting the public interest.

2. How specific and comprehensive is this code?

Although the code refers to various important ethical issues, its discussions are extremely brief. The code states goals—producing high-quality work, respecting cultural variety, etc.—without defining terms or discussing the complexity of such goals. The code is reasonably comprehensive, although it does not address complex intellectual-property issues related to digital information.

3. How enforceable is this code? How could it be made more enforceable?

The code is not enforceable. There is no procedure for investigating allegations of unethical practice. For the code to be enforceable, the STC would need to establish some sort of body that hears allegations, rules on them, and enforces penalties.

E. Suggestions for Responding to the Exercises, Projects, and Cases in the Book

Exercise 1. It would be unethical to lie to or mislead the potential employer by suggesting that you are interested in a full-time, continuing position. Simply tell the truth: "At this point, I plan to return to college in the fall; therefore, if you are interested in considering someone who is likely to stay only for the summer, please let me know."

Project 2. Although responses will vary, successful responses will do more than summarize the unethical article or advertisement. They will refer to multiple ethical principles presented in the chapter and provide specific examples from the unethical article or ad to support and illustrate the student's analysis.

Project 3. Since many students are unaware of their college or university's code of conduct, this project serves not only as a good opportunity to discuss codes of conduct but also as a good occasion to introduce students to a code of conduct they are currently required to follow. Successful responses will thoughtfully address the questions raised in the assignment. While not specifically prompted to do so, many students will refer to the three major characteristics of an effective code presented in the chapter.

Project 4. Although responses will vary, successful responses will refer to multiple ethical principles presented in the chapter and provide specific examples from the company's code of conduct to support and illustrate the students' claims. In addition, successful responses will address in detail most if not all of the questions presented in the assignment.

Case: The Name Game
This is a challenging case because Denise McNeil cannot be certain that Crescent Petroleum would act prejudicially if the company were aware of the ethnicity of the principal investigator or the sex of the company president. For all Denise knows, her company has already been eliminated from contention simply because she is female. By deciding to submit a proposal, Denise is betting that any prejudice by Crescent has not already eliminated her. She now has to decide the appropriate amount of accommodation to make to the culture of Crescent.

In my view, it is appropriate for her to use a first initial rather than a first name to disguise the sex of her employee, and it is appropriate for her to "remove" herself from the boilerplate history of her company. My reasoning is that neither of these actions involves lying. Rather, these actions involve withholding unnecessary information. By disguising the sex and eliminating the story of her involvement with the company, Denise is choosing to offer less information than she traditionally offers, but she is not providing false or misleading information. What is most important, she is not acceding to what she perceives as a prejudicial attitude by being prejudicial toward her employee. In other words, she is not firing her employee or making her less valuable at her own company. If Crescent were to explicitly ask her about the sex of her employee or inquire about why she has the same last name that appears in the name of her company, she should tell the truth.

However, it would be inappropriate for her to tailor Mark Feldman's last name to disguise his ethnicity. Doing so would be lying. In this case, lying would be inappropriate because it would represent too great an accommodation of what she perceives as a potentially prejudicial reaction by Crescent. She would in effect become an accomplice of Crescent.

Alternatively, if Denise has an available person other than Feldman to run the project, it would be ethically permissible to assign this other employee so long as doing so does not work against Feldman in his professional career. Before making such a decision, she should discuss the matter with Feldman to learn his feelings about being replaced. If he objects—that is, if he wants to be included in the proposal even if that would decrease the company's chances of winning the contract—Denise should comply with his request. In this case, following Feldman's wishes would be the right thing to do (from the care perspective), as well as the smartest business decision. Maintaining his trust is more important than winning this one contract, if he has given McNeil no reason to doubt his professional competence and character.

Chapter 3. Understanding the Writing Process

A. Summary

The writing process in technical communication is essentially the same as that in other kinds of composition.

Planning involves analyzing audience and purpose, generating ideas about the topic, researching additional information, organizing and outlining the document, and devising a schedule and budget.

Drafting is the same process in tech comm as in comp. However, many technical documents are created using templates. Templates have advantages in saving writers time and helping them achieve an attractive document, but they can unconsciously encourage writers to organize and develop the document in a way that is inappropriate for the subject. In addition, readers see particular templates often and can reach negative inferences about writers who use them. Writers should, however, use styles, which help ensure stylistic consistency (and enable writers to create automatic tables of contents). Automated hypertext linking tools are a convenience for readers of online documents; Web-conversion features on word processors can save time, but they often create flawed code.

Writers must develop their own techniques for revising technical documents. The chapter presents three strategies for revising. The first is to study the document using a checklist. (I also discuss the advantages and disadvantages of using spell checkers, grammar checkers, and electronic thesauri.) The second is to seek help from someone else. The third is to usability-test the document. Usability testing is the process of conducting controlled experiments to determine how users interact with and work from a document.

B. Goals

By the end of the chapter, students should be able to do the following:

1. plan a technical document using the steps outlined in the chapter
2. draft a technical document using the steps outlined in the chapter
3. revise a technical document using the steps outlined in the chapter
4. apply the techniques and tools used by people who write technical documents

C. Teaching Guide

I have found that, although much of the advice in this chapter was covered in first-year writing courses, most students need a refresher. Many students simply have not worked out procedures for writing effectively and efficiently.

This chapter extends the basic discussion of the writing process by covering word-processing tools: templates, styles, spell checkers, grammar checkers, thesauri, hypertext linking, and Web editors. Because technical communication often involves creating complex collaborative documents that include many sections, students need to learn how to use word-processing tools. It is especially important to show students the limitations of the tools: templates tend to lock the writer into a certain organization for the document, spell checkers don't know whether the writer is using the correct word, grammar checkers often flag correct constructions, and so forth.

Traditional-Classroom Approaches

1. Additional Exercise: Drawing a Cluster Diagram of an Article (see TechComm Web) asks students to practice the skills necessary to generate ideas about a topic by working backwards on a front-page print article. (25 minutes)
2. Build on your students' existing skills by discussing the writing process they learned in their composition course and comparing it to the process described in this chapter. (15 minutes)
3. Use transparencies of sample templates available on your word processor to start a discussion on the strengths and limitations of preformatted templates. (15 minutes)
4. Discuss how to devise a schedule for a technical document. Planning a document with several deliverables, progress reports, milestones, and review stages might be a new concept for students used to writing academic papers the night before they are due. After the discussion, have students create a schedule for a current class project. (25 minutes)

Technology-Enhanced Approaches

1. Additional Exercise: Analyzing the Audience and Purpose of a Web Site asks students to analyze your college or university's Web site, focusing on its audience and purpose. (20 minutes)
2. Additional Exercise: Searching for Advice about the Writing Process asks students to search the Web for the phrase "writing process." (25 minutes)
3. Additional Exercise: Drawing a Cluster Diagram of an Article asks students to practice the skills necessary to generate ideas about a topic by working backwards on a front-page online article. (25 minutes)
4. Help students efficiently draft and revise by conducting brief tutorials on how to use a word processor's advanced tools. Tools discussed in the chapter include templates, styles, automated hypertext linking, Web editors, spell checkers, grammar checkers, and thesauri. Of all these tools, I have found students benefit the most from learning how to use styles. (5–10 minutes per tool)

D. Suggestions for Responding to the Interactive Sample Document

1. Which of the basic concepts of usability testing are most apparent in this opening section?

The most basic concept of usability testing is demonstrated here: test real users as they try to complete a realistic task. The opening section reflects the idea that "usability testing permeates product development"—the designers sought input early in the design process.

2. The testers **did not** say to the participants, "Can you find the help icon?" Why not?

Directing users to the help icon would have biased the test. The testers wanted the users to have to figure out what they should do next. Thus, the testers withheld any clues that would have encouraged participants to select one icon over another.

3. How does point 1 show the value of choosing test participants carefully?

The goal of usability testing is to discover information that the testers would not have discovered on their own. By choosing participants who matched the profile of intended users, testers learned that users would prefer the Question Mark icon, even though testers themselves—who knew more about the product—preferred the Faces icon.

E. Suggestions for Responding to the Exercises, Projects, and Cases in the Book

Exercise 1. Learning how to use the outline function is particularly valuable because it helps students see their documents on a macro level, increasing the chances that they identify and prevent problems in organization and development. The outline function is also a tool for quickly reorganizing a document.

Exercise 2. Although responses will vary, a brainstorming list should feature short phrases (not sentences) and will likely feature some ideas that do not belong. Freewriting will often have incomplete thoughts and questions without answers. In a cluster sketch, the movement from larger to smaller ideas is from the center to the perimeter. Conversely, in a branch sketch, the movement of ideas is from top to bottom.

Exercise 3

a. faulty coordination
b. faulty subordination: a single subunit under "insufficient memory"
c. faulty coordination

Exercise 4. This exercise is valuable because most students can use the journalistic questions effectively during invention. Although responses will vary, successful responses will identify the *who, what, when, where, why,* and *how* of the article.

Project 5. This exercise helps students practice thinking in terms of how audience affects the rhetorical choices that writers must make. In addition, it asks students to evaluate critically the templates available in software applications.

Case: The Writing Process Online
Responses will vary, depending on the 10 sites the group selects, but all responses should present brief annotations of the sites to enable students to understand their strengths and weaknesses. An effective response might address the following questions about each site:

- Does the site seem easy to use? Are the explanations clear? Are examples presented?
- Does the site include a search function so that students will find it easy to identify the information they seek?
- Does the site cover a wide variety of topics, such as help for speakers of English as a second language? Advice on how to use search engines? Advice on how to evaluate Internet sources? Advice on how to use a word processor effectively? Advice on how to work effectively in groups?
- Does the site have interactive quizzes so that students can test their understanding of the topics?
- Does the site have printer-friendly handouts that students can print from their computers?
- Does the site link to other online writing centers?

Chapter 4. Writing Collaboratively

A. Summary

Collaborative writing is becoming increasingly popular in business and industry, as well as in universities. Collaboration draws on a greater knowledge base and a greater skills base, provides a better sense of audience, enables people to share the responsibility for the document, improves communication among employees, and improves the socialization of new employees. However, collaboration also takes more time than individual writing, can lead to groupthink, can lead to a disunified document, can lead to inequitable work loads, can reduce the collaborators' sense of authorship, and can lead to interpersonal conflict.

Conducting meetings effectively is an important skill for all students. The first step is to set the group's agenda: define the task, choose a leader, define tasks for group members, establish working procedures and a method for resolving conflict, create a style sheet and a work schedule, and create evaluation materials. Collaborators should conduct efficient meetings by being punctual and ready to work, sticking to the agenda, taking good minutes, and making sure every member understands his or her assignment. Collaborators should communicate diplomatically by practicing the skills of effective listening, letting the speaker finish, giving everyone a chance to speak, avoiding personal remarks, avoiding overstating their own positions, not getting attached to their own views, asking pertinent questions, and paying attention to nonverbal communication.

In critiquing a draft, collaborators should start with a positive comment, discuss the larger issues first, talk about the writing (not the writer), and focus on improving the group's document, not on the group member's draft.

Collaborators should learn how to use the comment, revision, and highlighting features of their word-processing software so that they can e-mail files back and forth among group members.

Men and women communicate differently, and both sexes should be aware of and tolerant of the other's communication patterns. Similarly, people from other cultures often find it challenging to work effectively in collaborative groups in the United States. Therefore, collaborators need to understand the ways in which cultural differences can affect group behavior.

B. Goals

By the end of the chapter, students should be able to do the following:

1. describe the advantages and disadvantages of collaboration
2. conduct efficient meetings
3. critique a group member's draft effectively
4. use the comment, revision, and highlighting features on a word processor
5. identify gender differences they are likely to encounter when collaborating

C. Teaching Guide

Collaboration is often the norm now, not only in college courses across the campus but also in the workplace. Therefore, although teaching the skills of effective collaboration is always a challenge, students will probably already have been exposed to it in other classes or in the workplace.

I recommend that you make collaboration part of the course by having students work together on a number of projects. Almost all the exercises, projects, and cases in the text can be done individually or collaboratively. Obvious choices for large projects that work well collaboratively are instructions, manuals, reports, and oral presentations. In creating collaborative groups, try to make sure that each group contains both men and women, as well as nontraditional students. I also try to make sure the students have different skills; if several students are experienced desktop publishers, try to distribute them in different groups. Some instructors like to group students who share basic academic interests—for example, by having engineering students together in one group—while other instructors prefer to avoid such groupings. I am not aware of any research that suggests an advantage of one approach over another.

The evaluation forms included in Chapter 4 (also available in Forms for Technical Communication on TechComm Web) provide a way for you to evaluate each student's individual contribution to a group project.

Traditional-Classroom Approaches

1. Discuss students' experiences with past group projects in other classes. Next, discuss both the similarities and differences between collaboration in the classroom and the workplace. (15 minutes)
2. Ask students to brainstorm a list of collaborative activities associated with producing a technical document. (15 minutes)
3. Supply a flawed sample document and ask students to critique it following the guidelines in the chapter. (25 minutes)
4. Bring in a copy of a style sheet for a technical document and discuss the value of creating a style sheet when writing collaboratively. (15 minutes)
5. Provide time in class for students to conduct a face-to-face meeting. Ask them to submit an agenda before their meeting and a record of their meeting after. (30 minutes)

Technology-Enhanced Approaches

1. Additional Exercise: Advice on Critiquing a Draft (see TechComm Web) asks students to use the Internet to search for peer-editing guidelines and to add to the suggestions made in the chapter. (20 minutes)
2. Additional Exercise: Groupware Tools on a Browser asks students to determine whether their Internet browser has any of the groupware functions discussed in this chapter, such as synchronous chat, revision features, or whiteboards.
3. Conduct a brief tutorial on using the comment, revision, and highlighting features on a word processor and then have students practice using these features on a sample document. (25 minutes)

D. Suggestions for Responding to the Interactive Sample Document

1. What is the tone of the comments? How can they be improved?

The tone of the first comment and the third comment are offensive. The first comment, with the obnoxious "huh?" and the word "exactly" suggests annoyance and lack of patience. The third comment, with "it's basically useless," is also insulting. The other comments, which contain suggestions or questions, are more positive.

2. How well does the collaborator address the larger issues?

The writer of the comments does a good job in identifying large issues: the importance of justifying their choice of tests, explaining the evaluation scale they plan to use, and ensuring that the audience will know that the writers have selected appropriate tests.

3. How well does the collaborator address the writing, not the writer?

The writer does a poor job addressing the writing, not the writer. For instance, in the third comment, "What kind of scale are you using" is unnecessarily personal. The comment could read, "Should the scale be presented?" Or, at least, the comment could refer to the scale "we," not "you," are using.

4. How do the collaborator's comments focus on the goal of the document, rather than judge the quality of the writing?

The collaborator does not clearly focus on the goal of the document. Even though the collaborator is highlighting important areas that need revision, he or she does not frame the comments in terms of the broader goal. Comment two, for instance, could read, "Good, but I'm wondering if our readers will want to know more about the tests we chose so that they better understand how we evaluated the servers."

E. Suggestions for Responding to the Exercises, Projects, and Cases in the Book

Exercise 1. I like to familiarize students with these functions because I use them in responding to student drafts and assignments. I find it effective to give students a short, flawed document on which to practice the revision features.

Exercise 2. The key skill here is the ability to attach, send, and open attachments in an e-mail program to which students have access. Often your campus e-mail program will be able to easily handle attachments. To check whether students have mastered this skill, send them an assignment as an attachment and require that they e-mail you their responses as attachments.

Exercise 3. Although responses will vary, successful responses go beyond a mere gripe session and analyze the factors that led to the negative experience *and* suggest strategies for preventing this experience in the future. They also describe positive experiences and describe strategies that might be applied to other projects.

Project 4. Responses will vary. If students evaluate existing information, they might need to conduct a few brief, informal interviews (see Chapter 7, page 150) with international students to understand how useful the information is to the target audience. If students propose material for new pages on a site, they might want to visit the sites of other colleges or universities to research what type of information they have available for international students.

Case: The Reluctant Collaborator

You and Allison need to try to resolve the problem with Ken as soon as possible. When the three of you get together, you and Allison should try to explain to Ken the importance of everyone's participating fully in the project. In addition, you should try to learn whether Ken has a problem that he will soon be able to solve, or whether he simply doesn't take the project seriously. You and Allison should try to establish expectations for Ken to meet for the next phase of the project.

You should also be sure to document all your dealings with Ken, so that, if the group falls apart, you can provide the instructor with documentation about your efforts to work constructively with him.

PART TWO: PLANNING THE DOCUMENT

Chapter 5. Analyzing Your Audience and Purpose

A. Summary

Before beginning to write, writers should analyze their audience. They should distinguish between primary audiences (people who will be working from the document directly) and secondary audiences (people who need to be aware of the information in the document but who do not work from it directly). Audiences can also be classified into four basic categories: expert, technician, manager, and general reader. Beyond these basic categories, every reader has individual characteristics that writers need to consider: education, professional experience, job responsibilities, personal characteristics, personal preferences, attitudes toward the writer and the subject, cultural characteristics, document use, and the physical environment in which the document will be used. The chapter presents an audience profile sheet to be used in analyzing the audience.

Writers need to know techniques to accommodate the multiple audience. In addition, when writing for multicultural audiences, writers need to consider seven cultural variables that lie on the surface—political, economic, social, religious, educational, technological, and linguistic—as well as six cultural variables that lie beneath the surface—the focus on individuals or groups, the distance between business life and private life, the distance between ranks, the nature of truth, the need to spell out details, and attitudes toward uncertainty.

Along with audience, purpose forms the writing situation of the document. In most cases, writers can express the purpose of the document in a sentence containing an infinitive verb. After assessing the writing situation, writers should determine how it will affect the scope, structure, organization, sentence structure and length, vocabulary, and tone of the document. Writers should then plan a strategy by determining whether it is necessary to accommodate the multiple audiences and by determining the relevant constraints. Finally, writers should check the strategy with the primary reader to see that it is appropriate.

B. Goals

By the end of the chapter, students should be able to do the following:

1. recognize the importance of analyzing audience and purpose when planning a document
2. classify readers into primary and secondary audiences
3. write text to meet the needs of expert, technician, manager, and general reader audiences
4. identify individual characteristics of readers
5. explain the impact of cultural variables on technical documents
6. choose strategies for communicating more effectively with multicultural readers
7. define the purpose of a technical document

C. Teaching Guide

Audience analysis, a basic principle of rhetoric for centuries, is considered today by many researchers and teachers to be the bedrock of technical communication. The problem for you as a teacher is that many of your students will not have thought much about the concept because they have never had to consider it. Almost all their writing has been directed to a single, not a multiple, audience. Typically, that audience has been the instructor. Unlike real audiences, the teacher has almost invariably known more about the subject than has the writer, thus making the writing situation even more unrealistic.

Purpose can also be a challenging concept to communicate. Most students have had only one main purpose in all their writing: to show sufficient knowledge or skill to earn a high grade in an academic course. Students consider writing to be an audition, not a useful or necessary communication of ideas and information. In other words, you have to show your students that writing is not a hurdle but an integral part of their day-to-day work. Make clear that there are four approaches to the multiple-audience document situation (virtually every memo and report the students will write): a "simple" document that frustrates the technical people, a "detailed" document that frustrates the managers, different documents for the different readers, and a document that uses a modular structure to accommodate the different readers. Only the last approach is feasible.

Traditional-Classroom Approaches

1. Bring in several technical documents and have students in small groups consider the following questions and then report their findings to the group:
   a. What are the various audiences for this document?
   b. What are the various purposes?
   c. How effective is the document in addressing the needs of its audiences and fulfilling its purposes?

   For more details, see Additional Exercise: Reporting on Audience and Purpose on a Web Site (on TechComm Web). (35 minutes)
2. Bring in copies of the Audience Profile Sheet (available in Forms for Technical Communication on TechComm Web) and have students complete the form for a current assignment of a recent document they have written outside of class. (20 minutes)
3. Present a brief context for a technical document (for example, a hospital brochure explaining a CAT scan procedure) and then ask students to identify individual characteristics of readers by answering the questions listed in the guidelines on page 86. (25 minutes)
4. Distribute a short technical document, such as two pages from a user's manual, and ask students to speculate on the changes it would need to be suitable for readers from Japan or Germany. (20 minutes)

Technology-Enhanced Approaches

1. Additional Exercise: Reporting on Audience and Purpose on a Web Site asks students to determine the audience and purpose of a Web site by evaluating the site's features. (25–35 minutes)
2. Additional Exercise: Identifying Audiences and Purposes of Professional Publications asks students to consider the audience and purpose of various documents from their major fields of study. (25 minutes)
3. Additional Exercise: Using Audience Profile Sheets asks students to fill out audience analysis sheets for themselves and for their instructor. (30 minutes)

D. Suggestions for Responding to the Interactive Sample Document

1. How does the difference in the salutation (the "Dear Mr. Smith" part of the letter) reflect a cultural difference?

By addressing the letter "Dear Sir" rather than "Dear Mr. Kirisawa," the writer is using a more formal, group-oriented tone. In effect, she is representing herself and her reader as representatives of their two organizations, not as individuals.

2. Does the first paragraph have any function beyond delaying the discussion of business?

The first paragraph sustains the level of formality introduced in the salutation, thereby showing respect for Japanese cultural norms. The paragraph shows other characteristics of writing to this audience: it begins with generalities, includes personal references and small talk, and reflects a relatively small distance between business and private life.

3. What is the function of telling Mr. Kirisawa about his own company? How does this paragraph help the writer introduce her own company's products?

By telling Mr. Kirisawa about his own company, she is flattering him and showing appropriate respect. The point about his company's success leads logically to the suggestion that his company might need to purchase additional products to sustain their growth.

4. To a reader from the United States, this paragraph would probably seem thin. What aspect of Japanese culture makes it effective in the context of this letter?

This paragraph appeals to the Japanese cultural value of providing excellent service over the years.

5. Why doesn't the writer make a more explicit sales pitch at this point?

The Japanese culture discourages explicit sales pitches, favoring instead a more subtle approach that emphasizes the role of providing valuable service to the customer.

E. Suggestions for Responding to the Exercises, Projects, and Cases in the Book

Exercise 1. Responses will vary. When reviewing responses, pay close attention to the language used. Because many students are already comfortable with the jargon and technical terms of their field, I have found that some students have difficulty identifying these terms and defining them for a general audience.

Exercise 2. This passage is filled with idioms that would be difficult for the nonnative speaker of English to understand. I'd recommend something like the following:

Your technical documents are going to be read by people around the world. But most translation companies have too many clients, cannot translate into the languages you want, or are too busy to complete your job in time. What should you do?

Translations, Inc. translates documents, including computer documentation, into many languages. We use expert translation software programs that work very quickly. Then our expert linguists correct each document to make it accurate.

We can translate large and small documents. We translate quickly. Please telephone us today.

Project 3. Although responses will vary, successful responses characterize audiences using a number of factors discussed in the chapter. They also offer a more detailed description of the audience and go beyond brief descriptions such as "soccer moms" or "construction workers." Finally, they identify hidden persuaders and use them as evidence for their claims about the two audiences. Less successful responses focus almost exclusively on describing the ads.

Project 4. Although responses will vary, successful responses use the three criteria listed in the assignment and report the differences in how the site was perceived by group members. They also discuss differences in individual characteristics of readers.

Case: Planning an Apology to a Customer from the People's Republic of China
Although response will vary, excellent responses will pose a series of question that reflect the student's understanding of the range of cultural issues that will affect how he or she should respond to the situation. These questions might include the following:

1. Is Haiwang Guo a man or a woman? What form of address should be used in the inside address and salutation?
2. Should the letter begin with a general paragraph similar to the one about the seasons that is used in the sample letter to a Japanese businessperson on page 99 in the book?
3. How explicitly should I restate the facts of the case? I want to be forthcoming, but I don't want to embarrass myself needlessly.
4. Should I explicitly offer the reader some sort of compensation for the incident, or would that be insulting? If such an offer is inappropriate, can you suggest a better strategy?
5. Should I use highly formal language throughout the letter, or would the medium level of formality used in the United States be appropriate?

Chapter 6. Communicating Persuasively

A. Summary

Communicating persuasively requires, first, considering the purpose of the argument. Writers need to understand their audience's broader goals—security, ego reinforcement, and personal and professional growth—and work within eight sets of constraints: ethical, legal, political, informational, personnel, financial, time, and format and tone.

Crafting a persuasive argument requires understanding the claim-evidence-reasoning structure of an argument. The claim is the thesis writers wish readers to accept as valid. The evidence consists of the facts that support the claim. The reasoning is the logic used to derive the claim from the evidence. Writers need to use the right kinds of evidence, including commonsense arguments, numerical data, examples, and expert testimony. In addition, writers need to consider opposing viewpoints effectively and decide where to put the claim.

Writers need to avoid common logical fallacies (such as hasty generalizations, oversimplifying, and circular arguments), which can undercut the argument. In addition, writers need to consider whether portions of the argument might be communicated most effectively through graphics rather than text. Writers need to project a professional persona by being cooperative, moderate, fair minded, and modest in their arguments. Creating a persuasive argument is, ultimately, a matter of ethics as well as of rhetoric; writers need to be aware of the ethical implications of their arguments. Writers should be aware, too, that people from other cultures might bring different expectations to the argument, having different ideas about what constitutes effective structure or even appropriate evidence.

B. Goals

By the end of the chapter, students should be able to do the following:

1. identify and respond to an audience's broader goals
2. describe common workplace constraints and their effect on technical documents
3. write a persuasive argument
4. recognize common logical fallacies
5. display a professional persona in technical documents
6. recognize the important role of graphics, design, and ethics in persuasion

C. Teaching Guide

Persuasion is a difficult subject to teach, yet it is vitally important. In my view, a central problem of most student-written tech comm is an inadequate understanding of what constitutes an effective argument. Although much of the material in this chapter echoes the treatment of logical argumentation in first-year writing texts, the chapter does address the issue of working within constraints, which is not usually covered in the first-year approach to persuasion.

Traditional-Classroom Approaches

1. Provide students with more practice identifying logical fallacies by asking them to identify and label fallacies in examples you supply. You can find many examples by searching the Internet for "logical fallacies." (20 minutes)
2. Print a copy of the hotel's apology in Additional Exercise: Sorry about the Alarms and the Cold Water (see TechComm Web) and ask students to analyze it. What is the claim made in the argument? What is the evidence? What is the reasoning? Is the argument persuasive? If not, where does it break down? (20 minutes)
3. Present a brief context for a technical document and ask students to speculate on what constraints the writer would need to work within when planning the document. (15 minutes)
4. Print a message from a discussion list in which you are a member (or use a print memo from your files) and ask students to describe how the writer demonstrated (or failed to demonstrate) an attractive professional persona. (15 minutes)

Technology-Enhanced Approaches

1. Additional Exercise: Finding Other Logical Fallacies asks students to search for additional fallacies not covered in the chapter. (30 minutes)
2. Additional Exercise: Analyzing an Argument on a Web Site invites student to consider an argument that one company's product is superior to that of its competitors. (20 minutes)

3. Discuss the hotel's apology in Additional Exercise: Sorry about the Alarms and the Cold Water and ask students to analyze it. What is the claim made in the argument? What is the evidence? What is the reasoning? Is the argument persuasive? If not, where does it break down? (20 minutes)
4. Ask students to find a site in which the graphics and design contribute to the persuasive argument being made. Likewise, ask them to find one in which the graphics and design contribute to a less-than-persuasive argument. Have students report their findings to the group. (30 minutes)

D. Suggestions for Responding to the Interactive Sample Document

1. In this first answer, what strategy is the writer using in addressing an opposing viewpoint?

The writer shows that the opposing viewpoint (that considering race in admissions is unlawful) is inaccurate.

2. In this second answer, what strategy is the writer using in addressing an opposing viewpoint?

The writer shows that the opposing viewpoint (that the consideration of race will hurt a white student's chances of admission) is valid but very weak.

3. Study the writer's tone in this answer. What words and passages undermine the counter-argument?

Calling CIR a "special-interest" undercuts the effectiveness of the counter-argument because it implies that CIR does not have the public's interest in mind. Saying that CIR "doesn't really care how the University considers race in its admissions policies" undermines CIR's credibility by suggesting that it is hypocritical.

E. Suggestions for Responding to the Exercises, Projects, and Cases in the Book

Exercise 1. Although responses will vary, successful responses identify elements such as text of claims the company wishes the reader to accept, technical specifications used as evidence to support the claims, icons to help readers accomplish tasks, photos and backgrounds used to evoke specific feelings, and graphics used to convey technical and nontechnical information. They also use concepts from the chapter to analyze the claims being made and comment on the soundness of reasoning.

Exercise 2

a. hasty generalization
b. appeal to pity
c. oversimplifying
d. *ad hominem*
e. *post-hoc* reasoning
f. argument from authority
g. either-or argument
h. *ad populum*
i. circular reasoning
j. argument from ignorance

Project 3. Some students need help finding suitable documents for this assignment. Although responses will vary, successful responses describe a variety of different persuasion strategies. They include multiple examples from the sample documents. Many students incorporate the material on cultural variables from Chapter 5.

Case: Being Persuasive about Privacy
Right from the beginning, this statement is unpersuasive because the company presents an uncooperative persona. The writer states that the company's goal is to balance the benefits of e-commerce with the rights of customers. But wouldn't it be better to let customers decide how much of their privacy they would like to surrender? The assumption underlying this opening statement is that the company is entitled to determine how much of the customer's privacy should be surrendered.

The section called "The Collection of Personal Information" casually mentions that customer information might be used for marketing purposes. Apparently, the company does not enable customers to opt out of such marketing uses of their personal information.

The next section, "Collecting Domain Information," concludes with the statement, "This information is collected automatically and requires no action on your part." Customers are not concerned that they will have to do anything to provide domain information; they are concerned that a company is collecting information.

The section "Disclosure to Third Parties" implies that customers can opt out if they wish to stop ads from third parties to whom the company has given or sold their personal information. But most customers would prefer to be given the choice of whether or not to let their personal information be divulged in the first place.

In short, this statement is unpersuasive because the company appears to be placing its own interests ahead of the customers'. If the Lucent statement is accurate, customers are not given reasonable opportunities to limit the extent to which their personal information will be used for marketing purposes.

Chapter 7. Researching Your Subject

A. Summary

This chapter discusses narrowing a topic, performing primary and secondary research about it, and assessing the information. Secondary information is available in print, in online databases, on digital disks, on Web sites, and in online discussion groups. The basic research tools available are online catalogs, reference works, periodical indexes, newspaper indexes, and abstract services. Students need to learn how to skim sources, record bibliographic information, paraphrase information accurately, quote correctly, and summarize accurately. They need to evaluate information according to six criteria: accuracy, bias, comprehensiveness, appropriate level of technicality, timeliness, and clarity.

Next, the chapter discusses five techniques of primary research. Inspections involve recording data accurately and analyzing it. Experiments involve establishing a hypothesis, testing it, and analyzing the data. Field research can involve both qualitative and quantitative measures. Interviews are discussed in some detail, with specific advice on choosing a respondent, preparing for the interview, conducting the interview, and following up after the interview. Questionnaires are treated in detail, too, covering the different types of questions, including multiple choice, Likert scale, semantic differentials, ranking, short answer, and short essay, and methods for testing a questionnaire before sending it out.

B. Goals

By the end of the chapter, students should be able to do the following:

1. narrow a topic to meet an audience's needs
2. choose appropriate research media based on topic and audience's needs
3. use basic research tools such as online catalogs, reference works, periodical indexes, newspaper indexes, and abstract services
4. employ paraphrases, quotes, and summaries as evidence in persuasive technical documents
5. judge sources found either in print or on the Web
6. describe the six major types of primary research
7. conduct an interview
8. collect data using a questionnaire

C. Teaching Guide

I know many excellent technical students who have not used the campus library since they had to write their term papers in first-year English. An excellent senior chemistry major might never have heard of *Chemical Abstracts*. Teaching how to find and use technical information is not easy. Trying to tell students about the hundreds of available resources doesn't work; they will listen as you describe the first few, but after a short while frustration sets in. They wonder how they will be able to deal with so much information. The guidelines on narrowing a topic suggest strategies to help students sufficiently focus their topic so that they can find useful information that will meet their audience's needs. I also suggest trying to limit the discussion of resources to a few basic tools, such as the Web, Kieft's (formerly Sheehy's) guide to reference works, a few of the basic indexes and abstract journals, and online databases.

The best way to introduce students to questionnaires and personal interviews is to have them try out these techniques on their fellow students. They will quickly get a sense of how difficult it is to write effective questions when they try to tabulate the responses and find that a good percentage of their readers misunderstood what the question was intended to elicit. Personal interviews can be practiced on students who have an area of expertise such as consumer electronics, sailing, or fly fishing.

The most important point, I think, is to explain the concept of doing research: understanding the difference between general and technical periodicals, using Web-based and printed accessing tools, and so forth. Describe the job of the reference librarian (often he or she is the best person to instruct students on how to use the library). Don't overlook what to you are basic points, such as why a report should refer to professional research, why the *Reader's Guide* is insufficient, and so forth.

The exercises in this chapter force students to choose their topics and carry out preliminary research. Using their responses to these exercises, you can help them refine their topics and steer them away from unpromising or excessively difficult topics. Inevitably, some students will come up blank and claim they have nothing to write about. Explain to these students how to use magazines such as *Time* or *Newsweek* as sources for ideas. If a number of students seem to be having problems choosing a topic, you might devote a half-hour of class time to showing two or three students how they can turn their course work or outside interests into effective topics.

<u>Traditional-Classroom Approaches</u>

1. Additional Exercise: Revising Questionnaire Questions (see TechComm Web) provides a gallery of sample questionnaires. Print a few examples and ask students to evaluate the effectiveness of the questionnaires. (20 minutes)

2. Additional Exercise: Comparing and Contrasting Interview Questions provides interview questions to be used by CPAs. Print a few examples and ask students to contrast the types of questions and evaluate the effectiveness of the questions. (20 minutes)
3. Bring in samples of broad topics and discuss the process of narrowing the focus of a topic to meet an audience's needs. (20 minutes)
4. Give students a page or two from an article written for a specific audience and ask students to paraphrase and summarize the information. In addition, ask them to write a paragraph or two about the article in which they integrate quotes from the article with their own text. (35 minutes)
5. Present students with a technical topic and have them discuss strategies for using search engines to find information. Include a discussion of advanced search features such as whole-language queries, Boolean operators, and wild cards. (15 minutes)
6. Take your class on a field trip to your college or university's library. Schedule a tour and a presentation that explains which print references and online databases are available to your students. (50–75 minutes)

Technology-Enhanced Approaches

1. Additional Exercise: Accessing and Using Online Databases invites students to learn more about how to access their library's online research databases. (20 minutes)
2. Additional Exercise: Comparing and Contrasting Search Engine Hits asks students to compare search engines and the types of hits delivered in order to learn more about effective search strategies. (15 minutes)
3. Additional Exercise: Comparing and Contrasting Usenet Newsgroups introduces students to newsgroups in their field of study. (15 minutes)
4. Additional Exercise: Evaluating Course Evaluations asks students to evaluate the effectiveness of two online questionnaires. (15 minutes)
5. Have students complete the tutorial "Evaluating Online Sources" on TechComm Web. (30 minutes)

D. Suggestions for Responding to the Interactive Sample Document

1. What is the publishing body for this site? Is it reputable? Is the information within the realm of the publishing body's expertise?

The publishing body for this site, the Insurance Institute for Highway Safety, Highway Loss Data Institute, is a very reputable organization. (You might need to do some research to determine whether a publishing body is reputable.) The information provided here is within the realm of the organization's expertise.

2. How can the information be verified?

Readers can verify the information by reading the article by Zador and colleagues cited in the footnote.

3. How timely is the information?

Because the article cited was published in 2000, the information presented here must have been written no earlier than 2000.

E. Suggestions for Responding to the Exercises, Projects, and Cases in the Book

Exercise 1. Although some search engines today claim to be able to rate the quality of a site, I have not found the claim to be valid; quality is too subjective a notion. This exercise works well when combined with the tutorial "Evaluating Online Sources" on TechComm Web.

Exercise 2. Responses will vary. This exercise provides students with an opportunity to learn more about the major sources of information and research in their major field of study. It also introduces them to the major issues discussed by professionals in the field.

Exercise 3

a. The question is too broad.
b. The question is too closed-ended and poses an either-or option that might not be appropriate.
c. Objection, Your Honor, counsel is leading the witness.
d. The interviewer should have found out this information beforehand.
e. The question is too broad.

Exercise 4

a. The subject is likely to be too complex for a simple yes-no answer.
b. The question is too broad for a brief answer.
c. A Likert-scale question would get at this information much more effectively.
d. This question includes a common error: How does a respondent answer if there are 10 employees or 15?
e. The instructions are unclear. Is the respondent to check off only one of the three or rank them?

Project 5. Although responses will vary, successful responses use a number of sources for information and support claims with specific examples. Some students might appreciate tips on how to improve the likelihood that a Webmaster will reply to their e-mail message (see Chapter 15, page 381).

Project 6. Responses will vary. Like Exercise 2, this project introduces students to the major print sources of research in their fields.

Case: Projecting a Credible Image for Your Organization

If you have not had a lot of experience with Web design, you might want to study Mike Markel's tutorial "Designing for the Web" (see TechComm Web) before responding to this case. This Web site presents a mixed message to visitors. On the one hand, the International Society for Microbial Ecology seems like a very credible organization. It is sponsored by a reputable university, and it is associated with reputable journals and professional conferences. In addition, the tone of the text on the site is open and inviting. On the other hand, the design and execution of the site are amateurish. The clip art is embarrassing, the typography pedestrian, the design busy and sometimes hard to follow. The tables on the home page, with their beveled edges, are unsophisticated. The overuse of colors is unattractive. All in all, aesthetics detract from what otherwise would be an impressive site.

Chapter 8. Organizing Your Information

A. Summary

This chapter covers eight basic organizational patterns used in developing arguments: chronological, spatial, general to specific, more important to less important, comparison and contrast, classification and partition, problem-methods-solution, and cause and effect.

The more-important-to-less-important pattern is useful when the discussion cannot be organized effectively using a chronological, spatial, or other similar pattern, or when it is necessary to call the reader's attention to an important point right away. Effective comparison and contrast requires that the writer choose sufficient and appropriate criteria of comparison and contrast and then decide which structure to use: whole-by-whole or part-by-part. Classification is the process of placing similar items into larger categories so that they can be understood as a group. Partition is the process of breaking a single entity into its parts or elements. Effective classification or partition requires that the writer use only one basis at a time, choose a basis consistent with the writing situation, avoid overlap, be inclusive, and arrange the items in a logical sequence. The problem-methods-solution pattern is useful when the reader needs to understand the logic of a project that began with an identifiable problem, proceeded to methods of analysis, and then yielded a solution. The discussion of cause and effect centers on deductive and inductive reasoning. The chapter concludes with a discussion of introducing and concluding the body of a discussion.

B. Goals

By the end of the chapter, students should be able to do the following:

1. explain the basic principles of organizing technical information
2. describe the eight patterns typically used in organizing information
3. choose the best pattern of organizing information given a document's specific audience and purpose
4. effectively introduce and conclude the body of a document

C. Teaching Guide

You have probably discussed some of this chapter's material with each of your students during conferences. But the instructor who does not devote class time to these organizational techniques—on the assumption that the students have already covered this material in previous courses or that everyone knows it anyway—is generally disappointed when the major assignments come in at the end of the course. Your job is to try to show the students that techniques of organizing information are in fact central to tech comm as well as to all forms of expository discourse.

It is a good idea to have the students hand in at least one of the extended writing or revision exercises from this chapter. The advantage of focusing your students' attention on these organizational techniques apart from the document they are working on is that they will not be distracted by all the other aspects of writing it, not the least of which is apprehension about the grade it will receive.

<u>Traditional-Classroom Approaches</u>

1. Additional Exercise: One Site, Many Organizational Patterns (see TechComm Web) offers many examples of the organizational patterns discussed in the chapter. Print examples and ask students to identify and evaluate the organizational patterns used. (20 minutes)

2. Additional Exercise: Organizational Patterns on a Syllabus invites students to study and evaluate the organizational patterns used in a syllabus for one of their courses. (15 minutes)
3. Print examples of introductions and conclusions and ask students to use the revision checklists at the end of the chapter to evaluate the effectiveness of these sections. (30 minutes)
4. Present scenarios for several technical documents and ask students to recommend effective organizational patterns for each document. (20 minutes)

Technology-Enhanced Approaches

1. Additional Exercise: One Site, Many Organizational Patterns asks students to identify and evaluate different organizational patterns used on a Web site. (15 minutes)
2. Additional Exercise: Organizational Patterns on the Toyota Web Site asks students to study the different organizational patterns used on a Web site. (15 minutes)
3. Ask students to search the Web for 3–4 different documents all covering the same topic. Have them compare the introductions, conclusions, and organizational patterns and discuss what factors might have contributed to any observed similarities or differences. (40 minutes)
4. Using a few pages from a document from this class or from another, ask students to cut-and-paste only the topic (first) sentences from each paragraph into a separate file. Exchange files and have another student predict what information follows each of the topic sentences. Afterwards, have students discuss how accurate the predictions were and what this type of feedback suggests about their topic sentences. (30 minutes)

D. Suggestions for Responding to the Interactive Sample Document

For each of these four questions, determine if the question is answered in this conclusion. If it is, in which paragraph (or paragraphs) is it answered?

1. What are the main ideas communicated in the argument?

The first paragraph of the conclusion presents the main idea, which is then presented in more detail in the subsequent paragraphs.

2. What should be done next?

The fifth paragraph explains the need for further research.

3. How can the reader find more information?

The final two paragraphs explain how to find additional information.

4. How can we help you in the future?

Readers who seek additional information from the NIOSH phone or Web site mentioned in the final paragraph will learn how NIOSH can assist them in the future.

E. Suggestions for Responding to the Exercises, Projects, and Cases in the Book

Exercise 1. Responses will vary. This exercise gives students practice identifying different patterns of organization and shows how audience and purpose affect the organization of information.

Exercise 2. More than one pattern of organization might be appropriate. Following are my responses.

a. chronological
b. problem-methods-solution or cause and effect
c. classification and partition or spatial
d. cause and effect
e. chronological or cause and effect
f. cause and effect
g. more important to less important
h. comparison and contrast
i. classification and partition
j. problem-methods-solution
k. classification and partition
l. cause and effect or problem-methods-solution
m. spatial
n. more important to less important
o. classification and partition or spatial
p. general to specific
q. comparison and contrast
r. general to specific or chronological

Exercise 3. Responses will vary. See the chapter checklists covering the eight organizational patterns for ideas on what constitutes a successful response for each organizational pattern.

Project 4. Two organizational patterns dominate this background statement: causal analysis and general to specific. The causal analysis is apparent in paragraph 3, in which the writer explains the rationale for the department's issuing the new exposure regulations. The general-to-specific pattern encompasses the whole background, explaining what methylene chloride is and how it can affect humans. The full document goes on to explain the nature of the substance in greater detail. This is a very effective statement of the background on the substance and the decision to revise government standards on exposure to it.

Case: Introducing a Document

The Web-based document excerpted here provides sufficient information for students to create an effective introduction. Here is a version of that introduction:

> The following OSHA Standard is related to employee exposure to methylene chloride (also called dichloromethane), a volatile, colorless liquid often used in industrial processes. The purpose of this standard is to help employers understand their responsibilities in protecting workers from dangerous exposure to methylene chloride.
>
> The standard begins with a background section that describes methylene chloride and its medical effects on workers. Next, the standard identifies the legal background concerning OSHA's standard on methylene chloride.
>
> The standard itself begins with the specific provisions regarding exposure limitations, as well as the employer's obligations to communicate about the hazard and to monitor for employee exposure. Next, the standard describes methods of compliance that employers must follow regarding control measures, respiratory protection, hygiene facilities, protective clothing, recordkeeping, and information and training. The standard concludes by directing readers to other sources of assistance from OSHA and from the various state governments.

PART THREE: DEVELOPING THE TEXTUAL ELEMENTS

Chapter 9. Drafting and Revising Definitions and Descriptions

A. Summary

Definitions are a crucial technique used in almost all kinds of technical communication. Parenthetical definitions are brief clarifying comments placed unobtrusively within a sentence. Sentence definitions, more formal one- or two-sentence clarifications, follow the item = category + distinguishing characteristics pattern. An extended definition is a long, detailed clarification using such techniques as graphics, exemplification, partition, principle of operation, comparison and contrast, analogy, negation, etymology, and history of the term. Definitions can be placed in the text, a marginal gloss, a hyperlink, a footnote, a glossary, or an appendix.

Descriptions of objects, mechanisms, and processes are central to tech comm, even though they rarely constitute entire documents. As with any kind of writing, an analysis of the audience and purpose is crucial before the writer begins. Most descriptions of an object or mechanism have a three-part structure: a general introduction, a part-by-part description, and a conclusion. The general introduction describes what the item is, what it does, what it looks like, how it works, and what its principal parts are. The part-by-part description treats each major part as if it were itself a mechanism. In general, the sequence of the part-by-part description reflects the way the item works or is used. The conclusion summarizes the whole description, usually by showing how the parts work in concert. A process description is similar to an object or mechanism description, except that steps replace parts.

B. Goals

By the end of the chapter, students should be able to do the following:

1. explain the role of definitions and descriptions in various kinds of technical communication
2. use an understanding of a technical document's audience and purpose to select effective kinds of definitions and descriptions to write
3. write effective parenthetical, sentence, and extended definitions
4. identify the most effective place for a definition based on a document's audience and purpose
5. write a description of an object, mechanism, or process

C. Teaching Guide

Students generally have little trouble with parenthetical definitions. Sentence definitions, however, are more difficult because they require a more formal structure. In particular, many students find it difficult to choose an appropriate category. The problem is either that they cannot choose a sufficiently narrow category to make the distinguishing characteristics meaningful or that they are so used to sliding into the definition without a noun in the category ("A PDA is what is used . . .") that they cannot understand the concept of using a category. Extended definitions usually give the student little trouble because they are less formal than sentence definitions. If the student has a good grasp of paragraphing and understands the subject being defined, the extended definition will come fairly easily.

Descriptions of objects, mechanisms, and processes are often the culmination of lower-level technical-communication courses. But for more advanced courses, too, you should try to find time to treat at least one of these three closely related techniques. Not only are such descriptions the basis of so many kinds of tech comm—especially specifications—they provide compact and easy-to-teach lessons that enable students to acquire most of the skills they will need for the more ambitious writing projects later in the course.

Most students find it fairly simple to gather all the information they need to write an effective introduction to the description. Sometimes, however, they have trouble deciding just how much information their audience and purpose require. A related difficulty is that they sometimes answer the five questions mechanically in separate sentences (see Table 9.1 on page 206 of the book). The cause of this problem is easy to understand—they want to make sure all the necessary information is included. They worry less about the style of the description.

If students understand how to write an effective introduction, they generally have little trouble with the part-by-part or step-by-step description, because it is the same process. However, there are two problems that bog down some students. The first occurs when the student fails to distinguish major items from minor items. For example, the description of a bicycle contains an elaborate description of the seat—the material it is made of, the type of springs and other hardware, the method of adjusting its height, and so forth. The second problem arises when the student is unable to sequence the item-by-item description. Sometimes the writer fails to follow through on the operational sequence of the mechanism or process.

The conclusion of the mechanism description is simple to write. Watch out, however, for conclusions that don't match the item-by-item descriptions in terms of sequence or identification of major items.

It is a good idea to have the students hand in at least one of the definition or description exercises from this chapter. The advantage of focusing your students' attention on these techniques apart from the document they are working on is that they will not be distracted by all the other aspects of writing it. They will also be able to get immediate feedback on their efforts.

Traditional-Classroom Approaches

1. Additional Exercise: Evaluating Definitions and Descriptions on a Web Site (see TechComm Web) asks students to identify and evaluate examples of definitions and descriptions. You will need to bring print copies of a sample chapter. (20 minutes)
2. Additional Exercise: Evaluating Glossaries asks students to describe and evaluate definitions. You will need to bring print copies of definitions from several of the sites. (20 minutes)
3. Provide students with a list of a dozen or so typical technical documents and ask them to brainstorm a list of how definitions and descriptions might be used in these documents. (15 minutes)
4. Present scenarios for several technical documents and ask students to recommend effective definition techniques and location for definitions for each document. (25 minutes)

Technology-Enhanced Approaches

1. Additional Exercise: Evaluating Definitions and Descriptions on a Web Site requires students to use research skills learned in Chapter 7 and find examples of the types of definitions and descriptions discussed in the chapter. (25 minutes each)
2. Additional Exercise: Evaluating Object Descriptions and Additional Exercise: Evaluating Process Descriptions ask students to use whole-language queries to identify and evaluate examples of different kinds of descriptions. (25 minutes)
3. Additional Exercise: Evaluating a Description of Lost-wax Casting asks students to evaluate a process description. (15 minutes)
4. Additional Exercise: Analyzing a Description of a Computing Process asks students to focus on the importance of audience and purpose to the effectiveness of a technical description. (15 minutes)

D. Suggestions for Responding to the Interactive Sample Document

Table 9.1 presents six questions that should be answered in an introduction to a process description. Determine whether each of these questions is answered and, if so, where:

1. What is the process?

This question is answered in the first section: "What Is Food Irradiation?"

2. What is the function of the process?

This question is answered in the second section: "Why Is Food Irradiated? What Are the Benefits?"

3. Where and when does the process take place?

This question is answered in the third section: "How Is Food Irradiated?"

4. Who or what performs the process?

This question is answered in the third section: "How Is Food Irradiated?" Because a process description is not meant to provide step-by-step instructions, the third section does not discuss the role of humans in carrying out the process.

5. How does the process work?

This question is answered throughout the third section: "How Is Food Irradiated?"

6. What are the principal steps of the process?

This question is answered throughout the third section: "How Is Food Irradiated?"

E. Suggestions for Responding to the Exercises, Projects, and Cases in the Book

Exercise 1

a. Reluctantly, he decided to drop—that is, withdraw from—the physics course.
b. Last week the computer was down (out of operation).
c. The department is using shareware, software that the owner is making available for a nominal fee, in its drafting course.
d. The tire plant's managers hope they do not have to lay off (temporarily cease to employ) any more workers.
e. Please submit your assignments electronically—that is, as computer files.

Exercise 2

a. A catalyst is a substance such as an enzyme that helps a chemical reaction to begin or proceed.
b. A DVD player is an electronic device that plays DVDs, digital video disks.
c. A job interview is a meeting, usually face-to-face, between a job applicant and a potential employer to determine whether the applicant should be offered a position.
d. A Web site is one or more related multimedia computer files that a person can view on the Internet using a Web browser.
e. An automatic teller machine is an electronic device that lets bank customers make transactions such as depositing or withdrawing funds from their accounts.
f. A fax machine is an electronic device that enables people to transmit facsimiles of documents from one location to another electronically through phone lines.
g. An intranet is a private electronic network used by an organization for storing and transmitting electronic files.

Exercise 3

a. A thermometer is an instrument that measures temperature.
b. A spark plug is a device that creates a spark to ignite the air-gas mixture in a cylinder.
c. Parallel parking is the practice of parking a vehicle—sometimes between two other vehicles—so that it is parallel to the curb.
d. A strike is an organized work stoppage during regular work periods.
e. Multitasking is the practice of using two or more computer applications at the same time.

Exercise 4. In the first paragraph, this extended definition uses etymology and a sentence definition of holography. Throughout the rest of the passage, the definition relies on principle of operation.

Project 5. Although responses will vary, successful responses develop extended definitions logically and clearly. They use one or more of the following techniques: graphics, examples, partition, principle of operation, comparison and contrast, analogy, negation, etymology, and history of the term.

Project 6. Although responses will vary, successful ones identify and comment on one or more of the nine techniques listed above in Project 5.

Project 7. Although responses will vary, successful responses clearly indicate the scope and nature of the description, effectively introduce the description, include graphics identifying principal parts, provide detailed and appropriate information, and effectively conclude the description.

Project 8. Although responses will vary, successful responses clearly indicate the scope and nature of the process description, effectively introduce the process, include graphics identifying principal steps, provide detailed and appropriate information, and effectively conclude the process description.

Case: Describing a New Fighter Jet

As of this writing, the F-22 files are located in the Products and Services/Integrated Defense Systems section of the Boeing site. The main page of the F-22 description is full of company-specific procurement and contracting information; students will need to determine whether this information is of interest to their readers in this case. The best information, including graphics, is found in the sections called "background info," "technical specs," and "multimedia." Students will need to read and understand the "Site Terms" statement. This statement will give you an opportunity to review copyright basics with students.

Chapter 10. Drafting and Revising Coherent Documents

A. Summary

The chapter discusses how to use structuring units—titles, headings, lists, introductions, and conclusions—effectively. Effective titles and headings are specific and announce the subject and purpose of the text. Writers should avoid long noun strings, be informative, and use a grammatical form appropriate to the audience and subject. Lists are useful in tech comm because they help writers focus on the big picture, examine the sequence of the items, create a clear lead-in, and clarify their prose.

The chapter also discusses paragraphing. Paragraphs should begin with a topic sentence, which summarizes or forecasts the main point of the paragraph. The rest of the paragraph should support the point made in the topic sentence. Writers should emphasize the coherence of the paragraph through the use of selective redundancy, transitional devices, and demonstrative pronouns.

B. Goals

By the end of the chapter, students should be able to do the following:

1. write coherent titles
2. write effective headings
3. write coherent lists
4. describe the difference between body paragraphs and transitional paragraphs
5. structure effective paragraphs by using a topic sentence followed by support
6. use coherence devices within and between paragraphs
7. revise documents using a top-down approach

C. Teaching Guide

The material in Chapter 10 is likely to be new to many of your students because it raises issues not covered in previous writing courses: document design, headings, and lists. In a more general sense, students are less practiced in revising for coherence than they are in revising for cohesion (sentence-level matters). However, students generally find the material interesting and useful. With the introduction of revising for coherence, I also recommend that you emphasize the importance of taking a top-down approach to revision. Some students get so focused on revising sentence-level matters that they forget to examine the design and coherence of the whole document.

Traditional-Classroom Approaches

1. Additional Exercise: Making New Paragraph Breaks (see TechComm Web) asks students to insert paragraph breaks in a long paragraph. (10 minutes)
2. Ask students to write titles for a current assignment on the board. As a class, critique the effectiveness of the titles. (15 minutes)
3. Provide students with several paragraphs from a technical document and have them write effective headings for each paragraph. First, have them write noun-phrase titles. Next, revise them into question form, "how to," and gerund forms. Discuss how audience and purpose influences the form of titles. (20 minutes)
4. After discussing the top-down approach to revising a whole document, present students with a rough draft of a technical document and ask them to make recommendations for revising it. (20 minutes)
5. Bring in sample paragraphs from technical documents that would be more effective in a list form. Ask students to revise. If you do not have samples readily available, you might have to convert some lists to paragraph form to use as your examples. (15 minutes)

Technology-Enhanced Approaches

1. Additional Exercise: Identifying Coherence Devices invites students to identify in an EPA brochure the principles of coherence discussed in the chapter. (15 minutes)
2. Additional Exercise: Analyzing Titles requires students to locate sample reports on the Internet and then evaluate the effectiveness of the titles. (25 minutes)

3. Additional Exercise: Revising Topic Sentences asks students to revise a set of ineffective topic sentences. (15 minutes)
4. Additional Exercise: This Has Got to Be the Worst Manual asks students to find two examples of different violations of the principles of coherence in a recent winner of the Worst Manuals Contest. (20 minutes)

D. Suggestions for Responding to the Interactive Sample Document

1. In what ways does the topic sentence function as it should?

The topic sentence presents the main finding discussed in the paragraph. In addition, it is clear and easy to read.

2. Identify the transitional words or phrases. How are they used effectively?

Sentence 2: currently; sentence 4: however. These transitional words help readers follow the logic of the passage. At the start of sentence 2, "Currently" helps readers understand that this sentence discusses the present situation. In sentence 4, "however" helps readers understand that the alternative discussed in sentence 3 had problems that led the team to reject it.

3. Identify the repeated key words. How effectively does the writer use key words?

The phrase "storage facility" is used in sentences 1 and 2. The phrase "supply sources" is used in sentences 1 and 3. The word "needs" is used in sentences 2 and 3. The word "groundwater" is used twice in sentence 4. These key words anchor the paragraph, which is about whether to create additional supply sources that produce water to meet needs, or whether to expand the storage facilities so that additional supply sources are unnecessary.

4. Identify the demonstrative pronouns followed by nouns. How effectively does the writer use them?

There is one demonstrative followed by a noun: "this alternative" in sentence 4. This phrase works effectively because it sums up and refers clearly to the idea presented in sentence 3.

E. Suggestions for Responding to the Exercises, Projects, and Cases in the Book

Exercise 1

a. This title does not make clear whether the document is a recommendation or an analysis of a recommendation. I'd revise it to Forecasting Techniques for Haldane Company: A Recommendation.
b. This title is too broad: what about disc cameras? What kind of study is it? Is it a technical analysis, a shopper's guide? I'd revise it to A Shopper's Guide to Digital Cameras.
c. This title is insufficiently precise. Does the 10-year view extend into the future or the past? What kind of agriculture? What is the West? I'd revise it to Agriculture in the Western United States: A Summary of Major Developments 1990–2000.

Exercise 2

a. This heading is a horrendous noun string. A revision: Report Findings of the Multigroup Processing Technique Review Board.
b. It's too broad: what about the Depression? A revision: The Great Depression of 1929: Lessons for the New Century?
c. Insufficiently informative. A revision: New Challenges for Intensive-Care Nursing in the Age of Managed Care

Exercise 3. I'd revise the passage as follows:

Scientists are now working on three new research areas related to improving the environment:

- Using microorganisms to make some compounds less dangerous to the environment. . . .
- Using genetically engineered microbes to reduce the need for toxic chemicals. . . .
- Using microorganisms to attack stubborn metals and radioactive waste. . . .

Note two things about this revision. First, you can put the number—"three"—in the lead-in sentence as an advance organizer. And second, you should make the bullet items parallel. I like to repeat the "using" construction because doing so helps readers remember the logic of the bullet items even after reading the substantive paragraphs. Other writers would choose other constructions for the bullet items.

Exercise 4

Responses will vary.

a. One new initiative regarding privacy issues on the Internet is the Web Privacy Project.
b. Engineers at smaller firms earn more than engineers at larger firms.

Exercise 5. However, therefore, for instance, of course, therefore.

Exercise 6

a. hearing
b. measures
c. decision

Project 7. Although responses will vary, successful responses identify recurring annotations as well as one-of-a-kind annotations, comment on the differences between annotations and summary statements, and comment on the value of having a draft reviewed by more than one person. This project also illustrates how individual characteristics of readers affect responses to writing.

Case: Writing Guidelines about Coherence

The title of this short report is effective in that it clearly identifies the subject and purpose of the report. The overview section is effective in introducing the research, describing the disease, and explaining the benefits of the model tested. The two other headings clearly forecast the content of the passages that follow them. The topic sentences in this report are generally clear forecasting statements. The topic sentence of the third paragraph ("Some patients . . .), however, could be revised, because it does not contain the main idea of the paragraph, although it leads into it effectively.

Chapter 11. Drafting and Revising Effective Sentences

A. Summary

This chapter begins with a discussion of principles of structuring effective sentences, covering lists, sentence rhythm, length, strong subjects and verbs, parallelism, and modification. Next, the chapter discusses levels of formality. The chapter then discusses matters of word choice, focusing on voice, specificity, jargon, positive constructions, noun strings, clichés, and euphemisms. This section also discusses matters of conciseness, including advice on avoiding stating the obvious and using meaningless modifiers, unnecessary prepositional phrases, wordy phrases, redundant expressions, and pompous words. The section closes with discussions of non-sexist language and inoffensive language about people with disabilities. The chapter closes with a brief look at Simplified English for nonnative speakers and at preparing text for translation.

B. Goals

By the end of the chapter, students should be able to do the following:

1. write and format effective lists
2. describe the reason for placing new information at the end of the sentence
3. choose an appropriate sentence length given a document's audience and purpose
4. write sentences with prominent "real" subjects and "real" verbs
5. state the function of parallel structures in sentences and identify faulty parallelism
6. distinguish between restrictive and nonrestrictive modifiers
7. recognize misplaced and dangling modifiers
8. select an appropriate level of formality given a document's audience and purpose
9. write clear and specific sentences
10. write concise sentences
11. recognize and avoid offensive language
12. define the concept of Simplified English
13. explain how to prepare text for translation

C. Teaching Guide

Teaching sentence style in tech comm presents the same challenges as it does in first-year writing courses. Whatever techniques work well with first-year students will work just as well in tech comm. Make sure, however, that you emphasize the importance of the writing situation. For example, if a writer is addressing a lower-level audience, a series of relatively short sentences might be most appropriate even though the writer might personally prefer longer, more sophisticated sentences. Making a text easy to translate is likely a new concept for most of your students. I emphasize that by following a few simple guidelines, writers can save themselves time and their companies substantial money when their text is translated.

Note that there are over a dozen goals for this chapter. You might not be able to accomplish all of these in one meeting. I recommend you spread these goals over several meetings, integrating them with ongoing assignments and the goals of other chapters.

Traditional-Classroom Approaches

For approaches 1–3, you will need to print copies of sample pages from TechComm Web.

1. Additional Exercise: Analyzing the Plain English Handbook introduces students to "Plain English" guidelines and asks them to compare these guidelines to the material presented in the chapter. (20 minutes)

2. Additional Exercise: Creating a List provides students with practice in turning a paragraph into a list. (10 minutes)
3. Ask students to respond to the other Additional Exercises, which call for fixing sentence-level problems discussed in the chapter.
4. Present several documents written with different levels of formality. Ask students to identify the level of formality of each and speculate how audience and purpose influenced the writer's degree of formality. (25 minutes)
5. Present several flawed lists and have students identify the flaws and suggest revisions. (15 minutes)

Technology-Enhanced Approaches

1. Additional Project: Making a Passage Less Formal provides an opportunity to discuss how a writer's sentence style contributes to the formality of a document's tone. (15 minutes)
2. Provide a brief tutorial on using the track changes and version features of a word processor. Have students practice using these features as they revise sentences in a classmate's draft. (15 minutes for tutorial, 20 minutes for practice)
3. Assign students one or two flaws discussed in the chapter (for example, dangling modifiers or offensive language) and have them search the Internet for examples. Have groups discuss their findings with the class. (20 minutes)
4. Have students search the Internet for "Simplified English" resources and have them report their findings to the class. (30 minutes).

D. Suggestions for Responding to the Interactive Sample Document

1. These two paragraphs contain many prepositional phrases. Identify two of them. For each one, is its use justified, or would the sentence be easier to understand if the sentence were revised to eliminate it?

Sentence 2 contains at least two inappropriate prepositional phrases: "of the proposal" and "of the review process." The sentence would read better if they were eliminated: "Proposals that are late will not be included in the group reviews, which means that the review process might have to be postponed until the next fiscal year." The sentence is still too vague, but it's better than it was.

2. These two paragraphs contain a number of examples of wordy phrases. Identify two of them. How can they be made into simpler, clearer expressions?

In sentence 1, "Proposals that miss the target date" could be changed to "late proposals." In sentence 3, "We also ask that you not submit" could be changed to "Please do not submit."

3. These two paragraphs contain a number of examples of pompous words. Identify two of them. How can they be translated into plain English?

In sentence 2, "necessitate" could be changed to "require," or the whole sentence could be revised as suggested in the response to question 1. In sentence 7, "contemplating" could be changed to "considering." In sentence 3, "cognizant" could be changed to "relevant" or "appropriate."

E. Suggestions for Responding to the Exercises, Projects, and Cases in the Book

Exercise 1

a. The causes of burnout can be studied from three perspectives:
   - physiological—the roles of sleep, diet, and physical fatigue
   - psychological—the roles of guilt, fear, jealousy, and frustration
   - environmental—the role of the physical surroundings at home and at work

b. There are four major problems with the on-line registration system at Dickerson:
   - Lists of closed sections cannot be updated as often as necessary.
   - Students who want to register in a closed section must be assigned to a special terminal.
   - The computer staff is not trained to handle student problems.
   - The university has to rent 15 extra terminals to handle registration because the Computer Center's own terminals cannot be used on the system.

Exercise 2

a. If we get the contract, the personnel and equipment must be ready by June 1. Therefore, a staff meeting for all group managers has been scheduled for February 12.
b. The results of the stress tests on the 125-Z fiberglass mix will help us understand our time constraints. If the 125-Z is not suitable, we will have to find an acceptable replacement by the Phase 1 deadline.
c. In our frank discussion, Backer's legal staff offered no specifics on their goals for an out-of-court settlement. However, we feel that they do not want to have to go to court.

Exercise 3

a. Can you get me the surrender value on policy A6423146 by tomorrow?
b. We were surprised to learn that the program contains an error. Please ask Paul Davis to go through the program.
c. The supervisor is responsible for processing the outgoing mail and for maintaining and operating the equipment.

Exercise 4

a. The number of students enrolled in two of our training sessions has decreased.
b. I recommend the new CAD system on the basis of recent research.
c. The in-store demonstrations have increased business dramatically.

Exercise 5

a. Pollution threatens the Wilson Wildlife Reserve.
b. We will evaluate the gumming tendency of the four tire types by comparing the amount of rubber that can be scraped from the tires.
c. The size of the tear-gas generator has already been reduced.

Exercise 6

a. The next two sections of the manual discuss how to analyze the data, how to draw conclusions from the analysis, and how to decide what further steps are needed before establishing a journal list.
b. With our new product line, you would expand not only your tax practice but your other accounting areas as well.
c. Sections 1 and 2 introduce the entire system, whereas Sections 3 and 4 describe the automatic application and step-by-step instructions.

Exercise 7

a. The Greeting Record button records the greeting, which is stored on a microchip inside the machine.
b. This problem, which has been traced to manufacturing delays, has resulted in our losing four major contracts.
c. Please get in touch with Tom Harvey, who is updating the instructions.

Exercise 8

a. We estimate that over the past three years an average of eight hours per week have been spent on this problem.
b. Information provided by this program is displayed on the information board at the close of the business day.
c. The computer provides the Director with a printout that shows the likely effects of the action.

Exercise 9

a. If you follow these instructions, your computer should provide good service for many years.
b. To examine the chemical homogeneity of the plaque sample, we cut one plaque into nine sections.
c. The boats in production could be modified in time for the February debut if we choose this method.

Exercise 10

a. The learning modules were created by two professors in the department.
b. The biggest problem faced by multimedia designers is that users become anxious if they fail to see a button or if they are asked to create their own buttons.
c. If the University of Arizona cannot determine where to store its low-level radioactive waste safely, the federal government could terminate research grants worth millions of dollars.

Exercise 11

a. You will find most of the information you need as you document the history of the journals.
b. When choosing multiple programs to record, be sure to choose the proper tape speed.
c. During this time, I also cowrote a manual on the Roadway Management System and made frequent trips to the field.
d. I made mistakes.
e. When you arrive, come to the reception desk, where you can pick up a packet with your name on it.

Exercise 12

a. In appreciation of your patronage, we are pleased to offer you this gift.
b. An anticipated breakthrough in storage technology will help us make better products.
c. Over the next two hours, we will demonstrate the new speech-recognition system that will be introduced in November.

Exercise 13

a. The results won't be available for a month.
b. The fire in the laboratory caused $10,000 damage.
c. A soil analysis of the land beneath the new stadium revealed an undiscovered aquifer.

Exercise 14

a. Please submit your research assignment on paper, not electronically.
b. The suspect was caught and arrested right next to the scene of the incident.
c. The new computer lab contains both PCs and Macintoshes.

Exercise 15

a. Williams was accused by management of filing inaccurate trip reports.
b. We must make sure that all our representatives act professionally with potential clients.
c. The shipment will be sent on time if Quality Control approves all the latest revisions.

Exercise 16

a. The meeting of the corporate relations committee has been scheduled for next Thursday.
b. The research team discovered a long-chain polyether that is glycerin initiated and alkylene-oxide based.
c. We are considering purchasing a tungsten-gun SEM that is capable of digital imaging and that is equipped with a diffusion pump.

Exercise 17

a. We hope the new program will help all our branches.
b. If we are to survive this difficult period, we will have to stay alert and work hard.
c. DataRight will be especially useful for those people responsible for maintaining the new system.

Exercise 18

a. Laying off employees will improve our cash flow.
b. Of course, we will have more accidents because the training schedule has been shortened.
c. Unfortunately, the patient did not fully recover.

Exercise 19

a. To register for a course, you must first determine whether it will be offered.
b. The starting date of the project had to be postponed because the authorization from the Project Oversight Committee was delayed.
c. After you have installed DataQuick, please fill out and mail the question card.

Exercise 20

a. The project appears to have been unsuccessful.
b. Our company's success depends on factors that are difficult to predict.
c. The presentation was well received even though we received few comment cards.

Exercise 21

a. The module's complexity will make it more difficult for the operator to diagnose equipment-configuration problems.
b. The purpose of this aptitude test is to help you decide which major to choose.
c. Another advantage of the Alpha team's approach is that it can combine different kinds of interfaces.

Exercise 22

a. The instruction manual for the new copier is unclear and incomplete.
b. The software packages make it easy to create graphic displays.
c. We talk with our sales staff every day.

Exercise 23

a. This modern soda machine is to be used by the Marketing Department.
b. Our proposal is late.
c. Please put your newspapers and other trash in the cans located on the platform.

Exercise 24

a. Each doctor is asked to make sure to follow the standard procedure for handling Medicare forms.
b. Police officers are required to live in the city in which they work.
c. Professors Henry Larson and Anita Sebastian, two of the university's distinguished professors, have been elected to the editorial board of *Modern Chemistry*.

Exercise 25

a. This year, the number of women with lung cancer is expected to rise because of increased smoking.
b. People with mental retardation are finding greater opportunities in the service sector of the economy.
c. This bus is specially equipped to accommodate people in wheelchairs.

Project 26. Although responses will vary, successful ones demonstrate an understanding of the principles of sentence effectiveness discussed in this chapter. In addition, they use concepts from the chapter to characterize and describe the analyses and speculate on the reasons for differences in analysis. They also comment on several points of agreement and disagreement in the analyses. Finally, they evaluate the usefulness of peer review.

Case: Revising a Draft for Sentence Effectiveness

This draft was written by a novice writer. It contains many errors of grammar, punctuation, and style, including comma splices, number agreement, unnecessary expletives, subject/verb agreement, faulty parallelism, and meaningless modifiers. Perhaps the most effective way to improve this draft would be to change the whole text from third person ("the student") to second person ("you"). Doing so would untangle many of the awkward sentences and help the writer relax. She uses numerous affected phrases (such as "owing to the fact that") that result from trying too hard.

Chapter 12. Drafting and Revising Front and Back Matter

A. Summary

This chapter discusses the following elements of the front matter: letter of transmittal, cover, title page, abstract, table of contents, list of illustrations, and executive summary. The *letter of transmittal* is a letter addressed to the principal reader of the report, introducing its purpose and content. The *title page* includes a title (a good title that clarifies the subject and purpose of the report), the names of the writer and the principal reader, and the date of submission. The *abstract* is a brief technical summary of the report. Descriptive abstracts indicate the topics covered in the report; informative abstracts convey the important findings of the report. The *table of contents* should contain all the headings used in the report. A good table of contents uses type variations, indentation, and outline-style headings to show the different hierarchical levels of the headings. The *list of illustrations* is a table of contents for the figures and the tables in the report. The *executive summary* is a one-page summary addressed to the nontechnical reader.

Next, the chapter discusses the following elements of the back matter: the glossary and list of symbols, references, and appendixes. A glossary is an alphabetical list of definitions of terms; a list of symbols is a glossary of the symbols and abbreviations used in the report. An appendix is any section that follows the body of a document.

B. Goals

By the end of the chapter, students should be able to do the following:

1. describe the purpose, organization, and format of common front-matter elements and write each element effectively
2. describe the purpose, organization, and format of common back-matter elements and write each element effectively

C. Teaching Guide

Many of the elements discussed in this chapter are routine. The list of illustrations, list of symbols, and title page, for example, require little creativity. However, many of the other elements call for a broad understanding of the challenges involved in effective tech comm.

A major problem in tech comm is myopia: the writer fails to assess accurately the needs of the audience. This problem can show up as early as the letter of transmittal, which often devotes too much time to the methods of the study and not enough to the major findings: the results, conclusions, and recommendations. The abstract and executive summary are also touchstones. Many students (and professionals alike) have trouble understanding the difference between the two.

A skimpy table of contents is further evidence of faulty audience analysis. Students who fail to provide a full table of contents are overlooking the needs of the hasty reader. An inadequate table of contents is generally the result of relying too much on generic headings.

Traditional-Classroom Approaches

For approaches 1–3, you will need to print copies of sample pages from TechComm Web.

1. Additional Exercise: Analyzing a Letter of Transmittal provides a sample letter of transmittal and asks students to evaluate it using the chapter's revision checklist. (15 minutes)

2. Additional Exercise: Evaluating an Informative Abstract presents a sample informative abstract and asks students to evaluate it according to the textbook's advice. (15 minutes)
3. Additional Exercise: Analyzing an Executive Summary provides a sample executive summary and asks students to evaluate it. (15 minutes)
4. Present the table of contents from several different reports and ask students to consider the elements and their order within a report. Discuss the differences students note and what factors contributed to these differences. (20 minutes)
5. Provide students with a jumbled list of common report elements found in the front and back matter. Ask them to place the elements in correct order and to indicate which elements are numbered with roman numerals and which with arabic numerals. (20 minutes)

Technology-Enhanced Approaches

1. Additional Exercise: Understanding Prefaces asks students to compare an introduction to a preface. (15 minutes)
2. Additional Exercise: Evaluating an Informative Abstract asks students to evaluate a sample abstract according to the textbook's advice. (15 minutes).
3. Additional Exercise: Evaluating a Table of Contents asks students to assess a sample table of contents according to the advice in the textbook. (10 minutes).
4. Deliver a brief tutorial on how to use the section breaks, pagination, and table of contents features on a word processor. (20 minutes)

D. Suggestions for Responding to the Interactive Sample Document

1. How clearly does the writer explain the background? Identify the problem or opportunity described in this executive summary.

The writer explains the background effectively in the first paragraph by listing the problems the engineers have experienced with organizing and storing information.

2. Does the writer discuss the methods covered? If so, identify the discussion.

The writer explains the methods very briefly, as part of the paragraph "We researched the capabilities . . ."

3. Identify the findings: the results, conclusions, and recommendations. How clearly has the writer explained the benefits to the company?

The discussion of the results and conclusions is vague: the writer does not state clearly which of the technical criteria the HP PDA meets. However, the writer presents clear recommendations in the final paragraph.

E. Suggestions for Responding to the Exercises, Projects, and Cases in the Book

Exercise 1. This is a weak letter. The first paragraph is insufficiently precise in explaining the subject and purpose of the report. The second paragraph needs to list the concepts discussed in the report. The third paragraph is potentially insulting and fails to provide information to help the reader get in touch with the writer.

Exercise 2. This executive summary clearly explains the problem motivating the report, but it does a poor job presenting the other information that an executive summary calls for. It does not communicate sufficiently specific information to help the managerial reader know the main points of the report. The one fact about costs—that composting is currently three times more expensive than ocean dumping—does not help the reader decide what to do.

Project 3. Because students are asked to comment on which style they find more effective, responses will vary. Often it will be a matter of which style they learned first. However, students should comment on and compare typical elements such as date of access, date of Internet publication, sponsoring organization, descriptive phrases (for example, "Online posting"), address or URL, directions for accessing documents, references to specific documents rather than home or menu pages, subject line of posting, posting and archival statement, and punctuation.

Case: Planning for Better Front and Back Matter
The information in this document is generally clear, but the lack of some essential front matter makes the document harder to use than is necessary. There is no abstract or executive summary, and the table of contents does not present sufficient detail to be truly useful. The table of contents, for example, could name the appendixes so that readers can determine whether to consult them. In addition, the table of contents should present at least the second-level headings from the document.

PART FOUR: DEVELOPING THE VISUAL ELEMENTS

Chapter 13. Designing the Document

A. Summary

A well-designed page is attractive and easy to read. In addition, it emphasizes the important information. This chapter begins with a discussion of the goals of document design and page design. It also provides terminology for discussing basic design principles: proximity, alignment, repetition, and contrast. The chapter then discusses document-design concepts: size, paper, bindings, and accessing tools.

The discussion of page-design concepts begins with an explanation of learning theory and its relation to page design. Next, the section discusses white space, columns, and page grids. White space—effective use of margins, columns, line spacing, and justification—is an important concept in page design. Margins provide enough space so the document can be bound, or so the reader can easily hold the page, and they provide a neat frame. A multi-column format enables the writer to increase the number of words on the page, to reduce the line length for easier readability, and to use space effectively when placing different size graphics. Line spacing is used to increase readability, to direct the reader's attention to graphics, and to clearly signal the break between paragraphs. Grids are planning tools that help the writer visualize what the finished page will look like.

Next, the chapter discusses basic concepts of typography: typefaces, type families, case, type sizes, line length, line spacing, and justification. Typography helps writers emphasize information for readers and increase the readability of documents. The chapter concludes with a discussion of designing titles and headings.

B. Goals

By the end of the chapter, students should be able to do the following:

1. evaluate technical documents using the principles of proximity, alignment, repetition, and contrast
2. plan the design of a technical document based on audience needs and expectations
3. choose effective sizes, paper, bindings, and accessing tools
4. explain the principles of *chunking, queuing,* and *filtering*

5. use columns, page grids, and white space to design a document's page layout
6. define common typographical elements
7. apply principles of typography to design an effective document
8. design titles and headings so that they are visually distinct
9. describe the uses of rules, boxes, screens, marginal glosses, and pull quotes in technical documents

C. Teaching Guide

Teaching design is often fun because, although most students haven't thought about it much or at all, once they read the chapter and start to look for design elements they see them everywhere. Probably because of their great exposure to print advertising, students are intuitively aware of a wide variety of design strategies. Your job is simply to harness their energy and direct it toward page design in technical documents, such as reports and manuals. I have found that introducing the principles of proximity, alignment, repetition, and contrast gives students a vocabulary with which to discuss and evaluate the design of technical documents. It is simple to find examples to talk about: a few pages from some software manuals or government reports will show a wide variety of strategies—and a broad range of creativity.

Traditional-Classroom Approaches

1. Additional Exercise: Analyzing the Design of a Catalog (see TechComm Web) asks students to identify two aspects of a document's page design that they think are effective and two that they think are ineffective. You will need to print copies of the document. (15 minutes)
2. Additional Project: Analyzing the Design of *Technical Communication* asks students to identify accessing tools and instances of *chunking, queuing,* and *filtering.* (25 minutes)
3. Additional Project: Comparing Two Designs asks students to compare the design of *Technical Communication* with that of another textbook and discuss how the similarities and differences might be attributable to the audience and purpose for each book. (45 minutes)
4. Provide sample technical documents and have students practice evaluating design elements using the principles of proximity, alignment, repetition, and contrast. Have them locate both effective and ineffective elements. (15 minutes)
5. Provide a list of common typographical terms such as *leading, justification, type family,* and *case* and have students provide definitions. (10 minutes)

Technology-Enhanced Approaches

1. Additional Exercise: Analyzing Publication Designs asks students to closely examine a specific design element, such as use of columns. (15 minutes)
2. After students complete the tutorial "Designing Documents with a Word Processor" on TechComm Web, conduct a brief lesson on how to use the styles, columns, and header/footer features on a word processor. (20 minutes)
3. Conduct a brief tutorial on how to create rules, boxes, screens, marginal glosses, and pull quotes using a word processor. (20 minutes)
4. Provide an electronic copy of a few pages from a technical document and have students change design elements such as page layout, line length, line spacing, and typeface to meet the needs of a different audience or purpose. Ask students to explain how their design changes effectively address the needs of the new audience or reflect the new purpose. (25 minutes)
5. Ask students to compare the accessing aids of a printed technical document to the navigation aids of a Web page (see Chapter 21, page 557). (20 minutes)

D. Suggestions for Responding to the Interactive Sample Document

1. Describe the use of columns. In what ways do they work well?

The columns work well in that they enable the writers to present a lot of information clearly. In addition, they accommodate the graphic and the text box effectively and economically. If the page were designed as a single column, a lot of space would be wasted on either side of the graphic.

2. Describe the text justification. In what ways, if any, would you revise the justification?

The justification—ragged right—works effectively because the spacing between words is uniform, making the text easy to read.

3. Describe the size and placement of the graphic. In what ways, if any, would you change its size and placement?

The design of the graphic is a little bit wasteful. Especially on the right side, the graphic contains excessive space. In its current placement, the graphic cuts into the left and the right columns. I would move the graphic slightly to the left, so that it cuts into the left column more but does not cut into the right column. Doing this would place more weight on the left side of the page, balancing the text box in the bottom right portion of the page.

4. Describe the design characteristics of the text box. In what ways, if any, would you change its design?

I would not change the design of the text box. The pale screen gives it definition, and the typography is fine.

5. Describe the use of white space. Is it insufficient? Sufficient? Excessive?

The designer is trying to convey a lot of information on the page. The page is a little cramped. I would expand slightly the space between the columns and the border of white space around the graphic.

E. Suggestions for Responding to the Exercises, Projects, and Cases in the Book

Exercise 1. This is a valuable exercise because it helps students see that a particular template always carries with it an implicit audience and purpose. This exercise also reinforces the points made in Chapter 3 regarding templates: (1) templates do not always reflect the best design principles, (2) readers get tired of seeing the same designs over and over, and (3) templates cannot help you answer the important questions about your document.

Exercise 2. Although responses will vary, successful responses identify differences in such design elements as accessing aids, page layout, typography, white space, line length, line spacing, justification, and heading design. They also evaluate these elements in terms of audience and purpose.

Project 3. Responses will vary. This project illustrates that a reader's individual characteristics affect his or her evaluation of a design element. In addition, because people might read a document for different purposes, individual design elements have differing levels of importance.

Case: The Underdesigned Data Sheet
The main strength of this design is that it is clear and orderly. The typography is functional, and the header and footer are clearly separated from the body of the page. That's about all I can offer as praise. The full justification emphasizes the blocky appearance of the page and is tiring to read. The long paragraphs, unrelieved by headings, are also tiresome. Without studying the full range of documents, I would be hesitant to suggest headings to incorporate in a template, but from this one page I would suggest the following: use the first paragraph for a general description of the item, but use no additional heading for it. For paragraphs 2 and 3, I'd create a heading "Key Features." For paragraph 4, I'd consider a word such as "Operation."

Chapter 14. Creating Graphics

A. Summary

Graphics are effective because they are visually appealing and easy to understand and remember. In addition, graphics are much more effective than prose in demonstrating most kinds of relationships in tech comm. Effective graphics have a purpose, are honest, are simple and uncluttered, present a manageable amount of information, meet the reader's format expectations, are labeled completely, are placed in an appropriate location, and are integrated with the text.

The chapter begins with a discussion of planning, creating, revising, and citing graphics. Next, the chapter discusses basic principles of using color effectively, focusing on the need to use restraint, to create patterns, to use contrast effectively, and to take advantage of the meanings the color already has.

Graphics are used to illustrate four basic kinds of information: numerical values (tables, bar graphs, pictographs, line graphs, and pie charts), logical relationships (diagrams and organization charts), instructions and process descriptions (checklists, flowcharts, logic boxes, and logic trees), and visual and spatial characteristics (photographs, screen shots, line drawings, and maps). After describing each of these types of graphics, the chapter discusses techniques for showing motion. Next, the chapter discusses creating graphics for international readers. Finally, the chapter discusses graphics software, including spreadsheet graphics, paint programs, and draw programs.

B. Goals

By the end of the chapter, students should be able to do the following:

1. describe the functions of graphics
2. use the six characteristics of an effective graphic to assess graphics in technical documents
3. integrate graphics and text effectively
4. explain the process for creating graphics
5. cite graphics used in technical documents
6. describe each graphic discussed in the chapter in terms of its purpose and what it does best
7. choose an appropriate graphic based on a document's audience and purpose
8. create graphics for multicultural readers
9. create basic graphics using graphics software

C. Teaching Guide

One of the principal difficulties that both students and professionals encounter in using graphics is, ironically, a verbal problem: they forget to explain, in the text of the document, what the graphic means. This failure is understandable because you will have a difficult time finding a graphic explained adequately in most technical journals or even in many textbooks.

Surprisingly, many advanced technical students do not know the basics of drawing graphics—such as the importance of measuring the increments carefully on an axis or of beginning axes at zero if at all possible.

Be sure to warn your students about some of the design problems inherent in the graphic templates in spreadsheet software; they are full of chartjunk.

Traditional-Classroom Approaches

1. Additional Exercise: Evaluating Computer Graphics (see TechComm Web) asks students to discuss the strengths and weaknesses of several graphics. You will need to print copies of the graphics. (25 minutes)
2. Supply students with a list of graphics discussed in the chapter and have them draw thumbnails for each without consulting the text. Conversely, supply thumbnails of different graphics and ask students to label each. These assignments work best when students can collaborate in small groups. (25 minutes)
3. Provide students with data from an almanac or newspaper and ask them to create several different graphics for a specific audience and purpose. (30 minutes)
4. Bring in copies of a few pages from a technical document featuring a number of graphics and ask students to discuss how effectively the writer integrated graphics and text. (25 minutes)

Technology-Enhanced Approaches

1. Additional Exercise: Evaluating Graphics in a Brochure asks students to explain whether graphics in a brochure are effective in communicating information to the intended audience. (15 minutes)
2. Additional Exercise: Evaluating Graphics in a PowerPoint® Presentation invites students to analyze Microsoft PowerPoint® slides they find on the Internet. (20 minutes)
3. Additional Exercise: Evaluating Templates in PowerPoint® asks students to analyze the use of color in some of the templates available in Microsoft PowerPoint®. (15 minutes)
4. Conduct tutorials on one or more of the following topics:
   a. how to use the drawing and picture features in a word processor (20 minutes)
   b. how to create business graphics using a spreadsheet program (30 minutes)
   c. how to modify and create simple graphics in paint and draw programs (45 minutes each)

D. Suggestions for Responding to the Interactive Sample Document

1. How effectively has the designer used the two colors?

The very hot red seems to dominate the very cool gray too much. The red could be toned down so that the contrast between the two colors is still clear but the red does not dominate the gray so much.

2. How do the drawings of the child and of the elderly man help communicate the point?

The drawings are clever in that they link the two bars for the same year by showing the child and the elderly man interacting in a way that reinforces the bars' numerical relationship. In addition, the drawings subtly show that the child is much more flexible than the elderly man.

3. Create a rough sketch of a graph that communicates the text on the right. Should this information be communicated in words or in a graphic? Why?

This information could be communicated in a simple bar graph with two bars: one for each year. Perhaps this information is communicated in words rather than a graph because the artist could not think of an interesting way to convey it in a graph. However, the information would be clearer and easier to process in a simple bar graph.

E. Suggestions for Responding to the Exercises, Projects, and Cases in the Book

Exercise 1. Responses will vary. This exercise illustrates how data can be presented in a variety of graphics and that each emphasizes different aspects of the information. I begin this exercise by providing students with tips on how to best get data from the admissions department.

Exercise 2. Although responses will vary, successful responses use labeled geometric shapes (rectangles or circles) or pictorial symbols.

Exercise 3. Although responses will vary, possible graphics include the following:

a. bar graph, pie chart
b. 100-percent bar graph, line graph

Exercise 4

a. The disciplines should be grouped by general category—engineering or liberal arts—not arranged alphabetically. The title should make clear whether these figures are for a particular school, a state, the nation, etc. Percentage changes should be added for the 2001 and 2002 columns.
b. Because the reader views the area rather than the height of the figures, this pictograph is misleading, making the large figures appear much larger than they should. Also, the vertical axis does not begin at zero.
c. The slices are not arranged bigger to smaller, starting at 12 o'clock; they are not labeled horizontally; and they do not contain real numbers or percentages. The insurance slice appears twice. The title of the chart does not say what period of time is covered.
d. This is the wrong type of graphic; line graphs show change over time. The correct type of graphic for this information would be a bar graph or a pie chart. There are other technical problems related to the imprecise title and the labeling of the axes.

Exercise 5. Versions a and b are poor because of the unnecessary third dimension. Version a is hard to understand because it is difficult to tell the quantities because of the lack of grid lines. Version b is hard to understand for many readers simply because it is a segmented bar graph. The best of the three versions is c, because it is two-dimensional. But even c could be improved by indicating the units for the vertical axis and adding the exact quantities for each bar.

Project 6. Responses will vary. This project introduces students to the graphics software available on their campus and it encourages students to teach themselves new software skills. It also asks students to critically evaluate the graphics created.

Project 7. Although responses will vary, successful responses explain potential problems and follow the guidelines for creating effective graphics for multicultural readers (page 354).

Case: Evaluating Graphics on a Web Site
There are plenty of graphics on this site, and they are very effective. The file called Setting the Stage, with the drawing of the user's computer and the Web server, clearly communicates the point. The annotated screen shot farther down the file also works well. The designer appropriately and effectively uses tables for most of the other graphics. Tables are useful for text boxes and for examples of coding. For topics dealing with graphics, such as animation, the designer clearly presents examples of the different kinds of graphics, including animated .gif files. The structure of the information on the site is also effective: the designer presents a point using text, then presents an example. The only suggestion I would make is to create a bigger border separating the site's information from the oppressive ads on the site.

PART FIVE: APPLICATIONS

Chapter 15. Writing Letters, Memos, and E-mails

A. Summary

In letters, the "you attitude"—looking at the situation from the reader's point of view and adjusting the content, structure, and tone to meet that person's needs—is crucial. Almost all letters contain a heading, inside address, salutation, body, complimentary close, signature, and reference initials. Most letters also contain some of the following notation lines: attention, subject, enclosure, and copy. Most letters are typed in one of the three following formats: modified block, modified block with paragraph indentations, or full block. The chapter provides guidelines for writing four types of letters frequently used in the technical workplace: inquiry, response to an inquiry, claim, and adjustment.

The memo—a brief, informal, internal report—is a very common format today because it does not require all the supervisors' approvals necessary for modern reports. The identifying information of a memo includes the traditional "to-from-subject-date." The body of the memo should begin with a statement of purpose to help the reader understand what he or she is supposed to know or do after having read the memo. For all memos of more than a page, the purpose statement should be followed by a summary; together with the purpose statement, the summary acts as an executive summary of the memo. The discussion section of the memo should include substantive headings to help the reader. Any statements of further action to be carried out either by the reader or by the writer should be segregated at the end of the memo in an "action" section.

Writers of e-mails should use the appropriate level of formality, realize that e-mail is usually archived, and abide by common netiquette standards by using bandwidth economically, revising their e-mails for correctness, avoiding flaming, using the subject line correctly, making the e-mail easy on the eyes, avoiding forwarding e-mail without the writer's permission, and avoiding sending "me too" e-mails.

B. Goals

By the end of the chapter, students should be able to do the following:

1. project the "you attitude" in correspondence for the working world
2. recognize and avoid letter clichés
3. identify and accurately use the elements of the letter
4. describe the purposes of the four types of letters most frequently used in the workplace
5. write common workplace letters effectively
6. write effective memos
7. follow netiquette guidelines
8. write effective e-mails

C. Teaching Guide

The inquiry and the response to the inquiry require some skill. The inquiry letter calls for a subtle tone, because the writer has to flatter the reader without seeming obsequious. In responding to the inquiry, the writer must accept the compliment graciously and, if the requested information cannot or might not be provided, deny the request diplomatically. The claim and adjustment letter package also requires some subtlety. The claim letter must be accurate, specific, and restrained. The good-news adjustment letter must be gracious, clear, and upbeat; the bad-news adjustment letter must clearly explain why the adjustment cannot be granted and still attempt to create goodwill. A very difficult point for many students is the distinction between an expression of regret and an apology.

The memo is a challenging format to teach because although it looks so clear and easy to understand, in every class a healthy minority will have serious problems with it. The major difficulty is that students sometimes have trouble distinguishing the details of the technical process from the managerial implications. Another difficulty is that some students will confuse the purpose statement at the start of the memo with the purpose of the project they are writing about. Finally, some students have difficulty organizing a multilevel discussion section.

Students today are fully comfortable with e-mails; however, many students see them as throwaway communication and therefore do not understand the need to take them seriously by adhering to the netiquette guidelines.

Traditional-Classroom Approaches

1. Locate memo or letter guidelines from a few different companies and have students discuss how these guidelines differ from what is included in the chapter. (15 minutes)
2. Supply copies of business letters you have received in the mail (and as e-mail messages) and ask students to discuss the effectiveness of the letters. (15 minutes)
3. Provide students with a reasonably well-written letter or memo and ask them to revise it by replacing the clear language with letter clichés and the "you attitude" with a "me attitude." This is an effective way to discuss "you attitude" and letter clichés. (30 minutes)
4. Provide students with a dense memo lacking a purpose statement, headings, and action statement. Ask them to revise it. (30 minutes)
5. Visit the archives of a discussion list such as TECHWR-L and print some sample messages. Ask students to evaluate the messages using the netiquette guidelines (page 383) discussed in the chapter. (15 minutes)

Technology-Enhanced Approaches

1. Additional Exercise: Evaluating Generic Business Letters (see TechComm Web) requires students to assess how effectively a letter employs the "you attitude." (15 minutes)
2. Additional Project: Evaluating Your School's Netiquette Guidelines asks students to search their college or university Web site for guidance on how to behave online. (30 minutes)
3. Additional Exercise: Evaluating Claim Letters provides an interesting lesson in what to do (and NOT do) when writing a claim letter. (15 minutes)

D. Suggestions for Responding to the Interactive Sample Document in the Book

For an additional Interactive Sample Document for Chapter 15, see TechComm Web.

1. Byfield's original post was titled "An Ethical Question?" How effectively has Hart quoted Byfield before presenting his own comments?

Hart has quoted Byfield very effectively. He presents enough of the original to be clear, but the quotation is sufficiently concise to conserve bandwidth.

2. How professional is the tone of Hart's response to Byfield?

Hart's tone is very professional. His comments are restrained and professional, and he sticks to the topic, rather than going off on tangents. He focuses appropriately on the ethical issues raised by Byfield. In fact, he never addresses Byfield directly.

3. How effectively has Hart taken care with the quality of his writing?

Hart's writing is clear and correct, projecting a strong sense of professionalism.

E. Suggestions for Responding to the Exercises, Projects, and Cases in the Book

Exercise 1. Although responses will vary, a successful claim letter identifies specifically the unsatisfactory product or service, explains the problem(s) clearly, proposes a reasonable adjustment, and concludes courteously.

Exercise 2. Although responses will vary, a successful "good-news" adjustment letter expresses your regret, explains the adjustment you will make, and concludes on a positive note.

Exercises 3–4. Although responses will vary, a successful "bad-news" adjustment letter meets the reader on neutral ground (expressing regret but not apologizing), explains why the company is not at fault, clearly denies the reader's request, and attempts to create goodwill.

Exercise 5. The writer of the claim letter has a legitimate grievance, but he hasn't made clear what he thinks the company owes him. The first paragraph of the adjustment letter should not admit that the can of tuna fish actually contained a fly (for all the company knows, it did not). After the discussion in paragraph two of the hygienic methods the company uses, the writer should not imply that the claimant was lying about the claim. And the adjustment itself—the coupons for two cans of tuna fish—is stated very grudgingly.

Exercise 6. Bill might write an e-mail to Larry, or he might consider sending an e-mail to all the workers that Larry supervises. The sloppy writing in Bill's e-mail reflects poorly on his professionalism and makes the e-mail very difficult to read. His comment that he doesn't have the time to go into all the details now is unprofessional. He should tell Larry when he *will* be able to answer his question effectively.

Exercise 7. The writer of this e-mail must enjoy eating lunch alone. The writer obviously does not project a "you attitude" (page 365) or try to create a professional persona (Chapter 6, page 116).

Project 8. Responses will vary. This is a good project for students to complete before working on an extended collaborative project. Learning netiquette will help prevent some problems within the group and will also improve the quality of the e-mails they send to you.

Case: Dangerous Wrenches
This case reveals two problems: you need to make a full adjustment to all the retailers who are selling the old tools, and you need to modify your company's procedures to ensure that any safety problems reported to the company are acted on immediately. First, you should write to Handee Hardware, Inc., offering them immediate replacement of the wrenches, at no additional charge, with your company paying for the mailing or freight charges. Then you need to write a memo to your company president that describes the problem—that your company has been receiving complaints about a defect in the product but that nobody has taken action. You might volunteer to head a committee to investigate your procedures and recommend changes.

Chapter 16. Preparing Job-Application Materials

A. Summary

There are seven traditional ways to get a professional-level position: through a college or university placement office, through a professional placement bureau, through a published job ad, through an organization's Web site, through a job board on the Internet, through an unsolicited letter, and through personal connections. Résumés and letters communicate through their content and their appearance; they should have generous margins, clear type, a symmetrical appearance, and adequate white space.

The printed résumé should be neatly photocopied or printed; should be honest; should be free of errors of grammar, punctuation, usage, spelling, and so forth; and should provide clear and specific information. If appropriate, the résumé should be designed and formatted for scanning into a résumé bank. The typical résumé contains the following sections: identifying information (name, address, phone number, e-mail address), objective, education, employment history, personal information, and references. Electronic résumés are increasingly common. The chapter describes different kinds, such as e-mailed attachments, scannable résumés, and Web-based résumés.

The job-application letter, which is the first thing the reader sees, expands upon a few of the points made in the résumé. The typical letter has at least four paragraphs: (1) an introduction, which identifies the writer's source of information and desired position, states the writer's desire to be considered, and forecasts the rest of the letter, (2) education, (3) experience, and (4) conclusion, which includes a reference to the enclosed résumé, a request for an interview, and the writer's phone number.

Students should prepare for job interviews by studying job interviews, studying the organization to which they have applied, thinking about what they can offer the organization, studying lists of common interview questions, compiling a list of questions to ask, and rehearsing the interview.

For every hour students spend in a job interview, they need to do many hours of preparation. They should send a follow-up letter after having been granted an interview and after receiving an offer or a rejection from an organization. Finally, an increasingly popular way to search for a job is to create an electronic portfolio, a collection of materials including the applicant's résumé and other samples of his or her work.

B. Goals

By the end of the chapter, students should be able to do the following:

1. plan an effective job search
2. describe the best ways to look for a position based on their field of study and experience level
3. design an effective résumé
4. choose content that is appropriate, honest, free of errors, clear, and specific
5. pick the most effective résumé format based on their circumstances
6. use tables to format a résumé
7. prepare an electronic résumé
8. define the concept of selectivity
9. write an effective job-application letter
10. explain the steps to prepare effectively for a job interview
11. write effective follow-up letters
12. understand the purpose of an electronic portfolio and the steps to follow when creating one

C. Teaching Guide

Most students are willing to incur considerable expense to have their job-application materials typed and printed professionally, but they are much less willing to put a similar effort into their content and expression. One result is that both the résumé and the letter often contain basic writing errors. Be clear in telling your students that potential employers have little to go on in evaluating their credentials except the letter and résumé and therefore employers will draw the logical conclusion from a poorly written set of materials: the writer is either ignorant or lazy.

The typical résumé and letter are insufficiently ambitious for today's job market. Many students think it sufficient to show that they have the credentials for the job. If the ad calls for a degree in mechanical engineering, they say they have one—but they don't elaborate on courses, assignments, and the like. The point is obvious to you, but not to many students: a lot of candidates are qualified for the position, but minimum qualifications will not ensure an interview. Spend class time reviewing sample résumés and letters, showing the students how to improve an anemic paragraph or résumé entry. If possible, have students criticize one another's work, trying to find areas of weakness as well as of strength.

It is fairly easy to demonstrate the different kinds of electronic résumés; students are very interested in the process of electronic job applications.

<u>Traditional-Classroom Approaches</u>

1. Additional Exercise: Evaluating a Sample Job-Application Letter (see TechComm Web) asks students to evaluate a cover letter. You will need to bring copies of this letter. (20 minutes)

2. Bring in sample print and online job announcements and discuss with students how to focus their letter of application based on information from the announcement. (25 minutes)
3. Ask students to write a chronological résumé as homework. In the following class, have them convert their chronological résumé to an analytical résumé. Finally, have them describe how they would change their résumés to an electronic format. Ask them to discuss which format they prefer and why. (45 minutes)
4. Supply several examples of weak descriptions for positions described on résumés and ask students to revise them to emphasize results, skills, and accomplishments. (20 minutes)

Technology-Enhanced Approaches

1. Additional Exercise: Creating an ASCII Résumé provides students practice converting a traditional résumé to a popular electronic format. (40 minutes)
2. Additional Exercise: Comparing and Contrasting Print and Online Résumés asks students to analyze online résumés and consider how they differ from traditional résumés. (30 minutes)
3. Additional Project: Evaluating Advice from a Career Center asks students to critically assess the resources offered by a career center and to consider ways to improve sample résumés and application letters, using the principles presented in the chapter. (40 minutes)
4. Additional Project: Seeking a Peer Response to Your Job-Application Materials asks students to get feedback on their materials and to assess the effectiveness of such feedback. (20 minutes each for feedback plus 20 minutes for memo)

D. Suggestions for Responding to the Interactive Sample Document in the Book

For an additional Interactive Sample Document for Chapter 16, see TechComm Web.

1. In the Objectives section, why does the writer specifically name the organization he wishes to work for?

The writer wishes to call attention to the fact that he has already worked for the organization and suggest that he is interested in working only for that company.

2. What is the function of a summary section in this résumé?

Same reason: he wishes to emphasize his experience with the company's own processes, suggesting that he will be able to be productive from the first day he rejoins the company.

3. The employment section precedes the education section. Why do you think the writer decided on this sequence?

The writer thinks, probably correctly, that his job experience is more attractive to the company than is his college education. Notice how the writer stresses customer service even when discussing his experience in the hospitality industry.

4. Why does the writer use a first-level heading for the security clearance?

The writer wishes to emphasize his experience in the airline industry and the advantage that he would therefore have over most of the other applicants for the position.

5. Why does the writer place the education section so low in the résumé?

The writer believes that his college education is not one of his strong points in this application. I would not immediately agree with him. He probably could think of ways to make the college experience relate more closely to his career goals.

E. Suggestions for Responding to the Exercises, Projects, and Cases in the Book

Exercise 1. Responses will vary. This exercise helps students who are still a few years away from graduation learn what skills and experiences are valuable to employers. It also gives them a feel for how much demand there is for the specific occupation.

Exercise 2. Responses will vary. Some students need help finding appropriate job boards. This exercise illustrates the type of Internet resources available for job seekers. It also asks students to critically evaluate the effectiveness of online-résumé generators.

Exercise 3. This is an ineffective résumé. Students can easily point out its shortcomings: it has a spelling error ("backround"). The identifying information is incomplete (no area code or e-mail address). The personal data includes irrelevant information. The education and experience sections are undeveloped (he should expand on his education and on the relevant jobs and cut the irrelevant information). The employment section includes too much information on the unskilled jobs. Much of the background information is irrelevant. Finally, this student should include a list of referees, with full contact information.

Exercise 4. This is an ineffective letter. The writer should include the zip code. She should rewrite the first paragraph to give the reader a reason to consider her application. She should add information to the education paragraph to communicate that she learned valuable skills in college. She needs to expand the experience paragraph by describing her positions in more detail. She should fix the final paragraph so that she requests an opportunity to meet with the reader, not interview her. She should list her e-mail address to make it easier for the reader to get back to her.

Exercise 5. Although brevity is appreciated in the workplace, the writer should provide a few details to help the reader remember who he is. The writer should also use this opportunity to highlight his skills and how he could contribute to the success of the Engineering Division at Safeway Electronics.

Project 6. Responses will vary. This project is a good culminating experience for the chapter since it requires students to understand and apply nearly all of the chapter's guidelines and concepts.

Case: Updating Career-Center Materials

Responses will vary depending on the materials already on the student's career center site. Students will find many hundreds of useful sites just by searching for keywords such as *resume tips* or *job letters*. (Links to a number of the best sites are listed in the Links Library for Chapter 16 on TechComm Web.) Another valuable resource is other college and university career centers, many of which have lists of links. Whether students decide to integrate new information with information already on their career center's site depends on the quality and scope of the career center's existing information. If the existing information is incomplete or outdated, students might decide, in effect, to start over.

Chapter 17. Writing Proposals

A. Summary

A proposal is a document intended to persuade readers to carry out some activity. An internal proposal is submitted by the writer to someone within the same organization; an external proposal is submitted to a reader in another organization. External proposals can be further classified as solicited or unsolicited, that is, requested or not requested by the reader. The concept that links all proposals is that the writer must make it clear that the future benefits of carrying out the proposed activity will outweigh the costs. The proposal must demonstrate that the writer understands the reader's needs and is able and willing to fulfill the promises made in the proposal. Most proposals contain a summary; an introduction, which defines the background and the problem or opportunity motivating the proposal; the proposed program, a description of what the writer would actually do if the proposal were accepted; a statement of the writer's qualifications and experience; and any relevant appendixes, such as schedules, evaluation procedures, and budgets.

B. Goals

By the end of the chapter, students should be able to do the following:

1. explain the difference between external and internal proposals
2. explain the difference between solicited and unsolicited proposals
3. describe the two major categories of proposal deliverables
4. describe the readers' needs in different types of proposals
5. demonstrate their professionalism in a proposal
6. use storyboards to plan a proposal
7. understand the basic structure of a proposal
8. use proposal elements to persuade readers

C. Teaching Guide

The proposal is a challenging document in tech comm for both students and professionals because a good proposal entails actually doing a good part of the project—without any assurance that the project will be approved. The writer naturally wants to put in as little work as possible to get the go-ahead; the reader wants to see an answer to every possible question before approving the proposal. In student writing, the result is often that the writer fails to provide a sufficiently full account, especially in the problem statement and the proposed program.

Because most students have had little experience writing about business and industry, they are not used to thinking in terms of real problems. Although many students quickly realize that persuading someone to spend some money to fix a problem requires demonstrating that the problem is more costly than the solution, many do not. Too often the writer simply sketches in the basic outline of the problem—such as that shoplifting is a serious drain on the resources of retail business—without presenting specifics. (How serious a problem is shoplifting to our organization? Is it serious enough to justify even an investigation of available ways to reduce shoplifting?) In other words, students are unused to thinking in terms of a cost-benefit ratio. They think it sufficient to label a situation "a problem."

The proposed program, too, is often weak if the writer has not read the professional literature on the subject. In fact, relatively few students can conduct a reasonably thorough literature search, analyze the sources, and synthesize them in a coherent description of what he or she would do. The tendency is to rely on generalities: "Then I will determine the optimum load." How will the writer determine the optimum load? Why use that method?

Sometimes students will submit a proposal without any reference at all to secondary sources. More often, a bibliography will be attached, but the proposal will provide little or no evidence that the student has read any of the sources.

The proposal at the end of the chapter is a positive example. I recommend that you devote some class time to this sample (and the complementary progress report and completion report in the next two chapters) as the best way to teach this material. However, you probably should explain that this proposal is not a template that students must follow. Their own audience, purpose, and subject will call for different rhetorical strategies.

Traditional-Classroom Approaches

1. Provide a short RFP and ask students to analyze it. Have them consider the following questions: (20 minutes)
   a. Who is eligible to submit proposals?
   b. What type of projects (or topics) is the funding source interested in funding?
   c. How will submissions be evaluated?
   d. What are the submission procedures and what is the deadline for submissions?
2. Ask students to discuss the following ethical dilemmas: (20 minutes)
   a. You are writing a proposal to a funding source dedicated to advancing the science education of young women. Your organization would like funds to develop software for physics labs at a small private high school in your area. After looking at the school's enrollment figures, you discover that girls make up only 20 percent of the student body. Moreover, few girls enroll in the physics class. The physics teacher at the school says that since they really need the software you should not include the low enrollment figures in the proposal. How do you proceed?
   b. You are preparing the budget on a $1,000,000 proposal. You notice that the project requires heavy computer use. Although your computer is not the newest or fastest one in the office, it is more than sufficient for the proposed project. Yet, you would really like a new computer. A new computer would make you more productive and would save your company a lot of money. It would be easy to add another computer to the budget without anyone noticing. What should you do?
3. Distribute a sample budget and discuss with students the types of items typically included in a proposal budget. Discuss as well how to effectively format the budget. (20 minutes)
4. Supply students with blank copies of the storyboard template (page 441) and have them complete the form for a topic from their own proposal project. Have them discuss the strengths and limitations of using storyboards during the writing process. (30 minutes)

Technology-Enhanced Approaches

1. Additional Exercise: Contrasting Research Proposals and Goods-and-Services Proposals (see TechComm Web) asks students to study sample grants and explain the major differences between a research proposal and a goods-and-services proposal. (20 minutes)
2. Additional Project: Assessing Proposal-Consulting Sites asks students to evaluate sites on the bases of clarity, ease of navigation, and professional appearance.
3. Additional Project: Comparing and Contrasting Sample Proposals invites students to review a number of sample proposals, noting the similarities and differences among them and describing, as well, any similarities to or differences from the proposals discussed in Chapter 17. (40 minutes for research plus 40–60 minutes for the memo)

4. Additional Project: Analyzing Characteristics of a Proposal from a Non-Profit Organization requires students to evaluate a full-length proposal. (20 minutes for discussion plus 40–60 minutes for the memo)

D. Suggestions for Responding to the Interactive Sample Document in the Book
For an additional Interactive Sample Document for Chapter 17, see TechComm Web.

1. Beginning in the second sentence of this paragraph, the writer describes the reader's own organization. What is the function of this description?

The writer is showing that she is familiar with the reader's organization and that her own organization's goals match those of the reader's organization.

2. The writer's description of the problem does not provide specific statistical evidence. Is this a weakness of the proposal, or is there a good reason for the lack of specifics?

In this instance, the lack of specifics is not a weakness. The writer presumably believes that, with her reference to the arrest demographics in Washington, D.C., and the similar problems in other cities, she has shown sufficient understanding of the nature and extent of the problem. In the interest of conciseness, she wishes to get right to her proposed program.

3. At the end of the solutions section, the writer refers to Attachment A, a task schedule. What are the advantages and disadvantages of attaching an appendix, compared with incorporating this information into the body of the proposal?

The chief advantage is conciseness: the reader can get through the body of the proposal in just a few minutes. The chief disadvantage is that, if the reader is skeptical, he might neglect to turn to the appendix, thereby depriving the writer of the opportunity to make the case that the methods she is recommending are legitimate.

4. Assuming that the reader is not familiar with CUP (the writer's organization), how effective is this description of CUP in establishing its credentials?

This section seems inadequately developed. The reader might expect to see a cross-reference to an attachment that contains more specific information about similar projects that CUP has carried out successfully, along with specific reference to the prominent scholars associated with CUP.

E. Suggestions for Responding to the Exercises, Projects, and Cases in the Book
Exercise 1. The NSF's Grant Proposal Guide provides some information on the best strategies for submitting a successful proposal, but the bulk of the very detailed guide concerns requirements regarding who may submit, what kinds of research the program supports, how to submit a proposal (down to how to staple the proposal), how proposals are judged, how projects are administered, and so forth. The reason for this level of detail is, of course, that NSF is a federal agency and therefore must abide by all federal statutes and regulations. For instance, the organization submitting a proposal must fill out a form certifying that it is a Drug-Free Workplace. The premium seems to be on scrupulous attention to fairness: every applicant must adhere to the procedures exactly.

Exercise 2. Although responses will vary, successful responses will focus on proof that the submitting organization is eligible, proof that the funding source might be interested in their project, award ranges, evaluation criteria, restrictions, deliverables, any special materials needed, signatures needed, deadlines (received by or postmarked by), submission procedures, and contact person for questions.

Project 3. Responses will vary. Writing a proposal for a research project representing a major assignment in the course provides students with a topic, an RFP (your assignment), and an audience (you). This proposal can be the start of a series of assignments such as a progress report, formal report, and oral presentation.

Case: Ethics and Proposals
First, you should study the proposal guidelines to see whether they address the question you face. If they do not, I think honesty requires that you notify the agency, telling them what your schedule is for naming a replacement for Martha Ruiz. The agency, not your organization, should decide whether and how to respond to the news.

Chapter 18. Writing Informal Reports

A. Summary
This chapter discusses typical kinds of informal reports. It begins with an explanation of the different kinds of formats used: memos, forms, e-mail, and letters. It then discusses five common kinds of informal reports: directives, field and lab reports, progress and status reports, incident reports, and meeting minutes.

A *progress report,* an undated version of the original proposal, communicates the current status of a project that has been started but not yet completed. The typical progress report contains four sections: an introduction, which explains the objectives of the project and provides an overview of the whole project; a summary; a discussion, which details the work already accomplished and speculates on the future promise and problems of the project; and a conclusion, which evaluates the progress of the project. A *status report* reports on the total activities of an entity in an organization, such as a department.

A set of *meeting minutes* records the logistical details of the meeting, provides an accurate record of the meeting, and reflects positively on the organization.

B. Goals
By the end of the chapter, students should be able to do the following:

1. explain the process for planning, drafting, and revising informal reports
2. list the four basic formats for informal reports
3. describe the purpose of the five types of informal reports discussed in the chapter
4. write an effective progress or status report
5. write effective meeting minutes

C. Teaching Guide
It is fairly easy to teach students how to write most of the informal reports discussed in this chapter. The progress report, however, can pose some problems for students. In the introduction, for instance, writers occasionally forget to identify the progress report as such; they simply start writing without telling the reader what kind of document they are writing. In addition, writers sometimes neglect to state the purpose of the project. Often, this is a result of faulty audience analysis: the writer has already stated the purpose in the proposal and therefore doesn't want to be perceived as boring by repeating it. Be sure to emphasize to your students that the reader will probably have read a number of other

documents since having approved the original proposal and might have forgotten the whole thing.

Some students don't understand what a summary is. Pay special attention to the summary section of the progress reports, because some of the writers who had difficulties with the summary earlier will still need some help. The discussion section of the progress report is generally structured according to time, tasks, or some combination of the two. Check to see that students are using a logical pattern and that they are using headings effectively to communicate that structure. The conclusion of the progress report requires a relatively sophisticated prose style, for the tone must be consistent with the facts the writer has communicated in the discussion section of the project. Make sure that students haven't overstated or understated either the problems or the potential promise of the project. Included in this chapter is the progress report that complements the proposal included in Chapter 17.

Meeting minutes are challenging to write in one respect: they require mature judgment about what to include and what to exclude, as well as how to be diplomatic in describing disagreements in a meeting. I haven't figured out how to teach mature judgment. Please get in touch with me if you have.

Traditional-Classroom Approaches

1. Additional Exercise: Status Reports and Progress Reports (see TechComm Web) asks students to consider the difference between status and progress reports and to make recommendations for improving a sample status report. You will need to make print copies. (20 minutes)
2. Additional Projects: Writing a Directive, Revising a Lab Report, and Revising a Set of Meeting Minutes gives students practice writing and revising three common informal reports. You will need to make copies of the documents to be revised. (20 minutes each)
3. Provide time in class for groups of students to meet and discuss a collaborative project. Ask each student to write minutes for the meeting. Have each student exchange minutes with another student in the same group and ask them to discuss how the minutes differ. (40 minutes)
4. Supply students with a short progress report organized using the time pattern (page 469) and ask students to revise it using the task pattern. (30 minutes)
5. Supply a sample incident report and ask students to evaluate it using the chapter's Revision Checklist (page 479). (20 minutes)

Technology-Enhanced Approaches

1. Additional Exercise: Looking for Report Guidelines asks students to search the Internet for advice on writing lab reports. (20 minutes)
2. Additional Project: Analyzing Purpose and Form in Informal Reports asks students to study several reports and to discuss how different purposes affect such factors as structure, use of graphics, use of quotations, and level of formality. (30 minutes)
3. Ask students to find an informal report on the Web and to evaluate the report using the chapter's Revision Checklist (page 479). (25 minutes)
4. Have students search the Web for sample incident reports and have them compare their findings to the sample in the chapter (page 477). Ask them to develop a brief set of guidelines for writing effective incident reports. (30 minutes)

D. Suggestions for Responding to the Interactive Sample Document in the Book
For an additional Interactive Sample Document for Chapter 18, see TechComm Web.

1. What is the problem that the writer is confronting in this portion of her progress report?

The problem is presented in the second sentence: "Unfortunately, the term *ruggedized* is used differently by different manufacturers."

2. How effective is the writer's tone?

The writer's tone is straightforward and direct. She presents a fact (such as that there are Milspecs), then the problem (such as that there are many, many Milspecs, none of which are specifically related to laptops). The writer comes across as a careful analyst trying hard to present the information clearly and accurately.

3. How honest does the writer seem in reporting her progress?

The writer appears to be very honest. This impression comes across in her willingness to state clearly that there is no fully appropriate standard for judging the ruggedness of laptops. A temptation that writers need to resist is the desire to present information in the most favorable light.

E. Suggestions for Responding to the Exercises, Projects, and Cases in the Book
Exercise 1. Although responses will vary, successful responses begin with a polite explanatory note and then explain the reasons for a new smoking policy for the showroom.

Exercise 2. This memo is flawed in several ways. It has an imprecise subject heading. It does not begin with a purpose statement, so the reader doesn't know what the writer wants him to know or do. The writer spends more time on the background of the situation—paragraph one—than on the actual message. The writer does not make clear exactly what she wants her reader to do or how he is supposed to go about doing it. Finally, the tone is awful: curt and condescending.

Project 3. Although responses will vary, a successful progress report clearly announces that it is a progress or status report, uses an appropriate organizational pattern, clearly and honestly reports on the subject and forecasts the problems and possibilities of the future work, and appends supporting materials that substantiate the discussion.

Project 4. Responses will vary. This project introduces students to parliamentary procedure and familiarizes them with what resources are available on the Web. I have found that knowing parliamentary procedure is a powerful tool for running efficient meetings in which all participants have a chance to be heard. Some students will need instruction on how to document Internet sources both in their text and in a reference list (see Appendix, Part A, page 592).

Case: Amending a Proposal
In your progress report, you should clearly explain your mistake and recommend whatever action you think would be in the best interests of the company: researching the third company using alternative means, or adding them to your itinerary. The main reason to do so is that it is the right thing to do: your supervisor needs to make an informed decision on how to proceed, and he or she deserves the benefit of your recommendation. Being truthful will probably not hurt you within the company; everyone makes mistakes.

But covering up the new information could come back to haunt you; some time in the future, people in the company are going to discover the third company and wonder why you did not visit them. Being discovered as an untruthful person *will* probably hurt you.

Chapter 19. Writing Formal Reports

A. Summary

There are three main types of formal reports: informational, analytical, and recommendation. An informational report provides data; an analytical report draws conclusions, and a recommendation report suggests future actions.

The chapter provides problem-solving models for formal reports and for one special kind of formal report: the feasibility report. For preparing feasibility studies, a useful model is to analyze the audience and purpose, then identify the problem or opportunity, establish criteria for responding to it, determine the options, study each option according to the criteria, draw conclusions about each option, and formulate recommendations.

The typical formal report contains many, if not most, of the formal elements discussed in Chapter 12. Chapter 18 discusses the body of the report. In most cases, the body contains five elements: the introduction, which describes the problem, scope, and purpose of the project; the methods, which describes the procedures used in carrying out the project; the results (the data that were observed, discovered, or created); the conclusions (the meaning of the results); and the recommendations (a suggested course of action).

B. Goals

By the end of the chapter, students should be able to do the following:

1. describe the main purposes of the three kinds of formal reports discussed in the chapter
2. use the problem-solving model for preparing a formal report
3. list the three kinds of questions a feasibility report can address
4. apply the steps discussed in the chapter to prepare a feasibility report
5. develop minimum specifications and evaluative criteria
6. organize the elements of a typical report effectively
7. include appropriate and persuasive content in a report's introduction, methods, results, conclusions, and recommendations

C. Teaching Guide

In this chapter, I pay particular attention to feasibility studies because many student projects take this form and students do not automatically understand its logic.

In discussing the introduction to the report, emphasize to the students that, because the report will be the official record of the project as well as an immediate working document, they must clearly explain the problem, scope, and purpose of the project. If a student raises the objection that all this information has already been explained in the proposal and the progress report(s), give the obvious answer: the reader is likely to have forgotten the information. A related question concerns redundancy within the report itself. Even though some of the material in the introduction was already covered in earlier sections of the report, the redundancy in the introduction is necessary for two reasons: not all readers will look at the other elements, and the introduction provides the most detailed and comprehensive version of this information.

The methods section of the body is the easiest section for almost all students because it covers the procedures—the aspect of the project the students are most familiar with—and because it most closely resembles the kind of technical communication with which they have the most experience: the lab report. However, in teaching the methods section, don't forget to remind students to justify the method they chose for carrying out the project and to structure the discussion according to a logical pattern.

The three final elements of the body—the results, conclusions, and recommendations—trouble both students and professionals the most. Point out to students that combining the results and the conclusions might cause readers to doubt that the results were achieved and recorded objectively. The recommendations should be numbered and expressed clearly and diplomatically. Warn students not to overstate ("I cannot understand why the company ever decided to use batch processing in the first place"). There probably was a rational reason when the original decision was made, and at any rate there is no purpose in antagonizing the person or persons associated with the original decision.

The formal report that complements the proposal and progress report in the preceding two chapters is included at the end of the chapter.

Traditional-Classroom Approaches

1. Additional Exercise: Studying an Effective Executive Summary (see TechComm Web) asks students to identify two techniques used in the executive summary of a report that help readers understand the major findings. You will need to print copies of the executive summary. (15 minutes)
2. Additional Exercise: Evaluating an Introduction asks students to use the Revision Checklist (page 519) to evaluate an introduction taken from a report published by the Environmental Protection Agency. You will need to print copies of the introduction. (15 minutes)
3. Ask students to develop minimum specifications and evaluation criteria (page 491) for some household item (for example, a computer, refrigerator, cell phone, and so on). After they write the criteria, have them exchange papers and discuss how audience and purpose affected the criteria. (25 minutes)
4. Provide samples from the results, conclusions, and recommendation sections of reports. Ask students to describe the different types of information each section contains. (30 minutes)

Technology-Enhanced Approaches

1. Additional Project: Different Structures in Formal Reports asks students to study the differences between reports written by NASA writers and the sample reports in the chapter. (25 minutes)
2. Ask students to search the Web for examples of specifications and evaluation criteria. Have them discuss the differences between the two types of information and develop guidelines for effectively writing specifications or evaluation criteria. (30 minutes)
3. Ask students to use the Links Library to locate a report on a subject that interests them. Have them identify persuasive language or other strategies that the writer uses to persuade readers to accept the report's conclusions or recommendations. (25 minutes)
4. Ask students to locate a report designed for online viewing only (for example, a paper or PDF version is not available). Have them describe the differences in design between the online report and the examples in the text. (25 minutes)

D. Suggestions for Responding to the Interactive Sample Document in the Book
For an additional Interactive Sample Document for Chapter 19, see TechComm Web.

1. What is the subject of the report? How clearly is it stated in this introduction?

The subject of this report—the link between risk behaviors and death—is introduced as early as the title, and then in the first two sentences of the introduction.

2. What recommendations is the writer making?

In the paragraph after the bulleted list, the writer clearly recommends that young people avoid these risk behaviors. However, the use of the passive voice in one sentence—"positive choices need to be promoted"—blunts the impact of the recommendation, because the writer fails to state clearly who should promote those positive choices.

3. What questions has the writer neglected to answer in this introduction?

The writer does not clearly state the purpose of the report, the sources of information, the scope, the organization, and the key terms.

E. Suggestions for Responding to the Exercises, Projects, and Cases in the Book

Exercise 1

a. Examples of minimum specifications: the printer must work with an Apple Mac, must print at least 6 pages per minute, and must have at least 600 × 600 dpi resolution. Examples of evaluative criteria: ease of use, durability, and cost.
b. Examples of minimum specifications: the major requirements must overlap with the courses I have already taken so that I can graduate in no more than five more semesters, and the major must have excellent job prospects within the city. Examples of evaluative criteria: whether the major is interesting to me and gives me the skills to do something that I think is important.
c. Examples of minimum specifications: the company must be located near public transportation and offer a salary of at least $35,000. Examples of evaluative criteria: the number of people my age the company employs and the quality of the product or service the company produces.
d. Examples of minimum specifications: the car must have four-wheel drive and be able to seat at least five people. Examples of evaluative criteria: the age of the car and the number of miles it has been driven.
e. Examples of minimum specifications: the place to live must be located less than one mile from campus and cost less than $400 per month, including utilities. Examples of evaluative criteria: the number of people my age who live there and the attractiveness of the place.

Exercise 2. Responses will vary. This exercise illustrates to students that there is no one single format for a report and no one agreed-upon set of elements. Such differences are a reflection of the audience, purpose, and subject of individual reports.

Project 3. Although responses will vary, successful completion reports adhere to the guidelines reflected in the Revision Checklist (page 519).

Project 4. Responses will vary. I encourage students to use the Revision Checklist (page 519) as they evaluate the report.

Case: Turning a Letter into a Report

I would use the following headings:

On page 1: The Presidential Directives to Improve the Department of Energy's Voluntary Reporting of Greenhouse Gases Program

At the bottom of page 2: Actions Already Taken by the Department of Energy

At the top of page 4: Suggested Changes to the Voluntary Reporting of Greenhouse Gases Program

Chapter 20. Writing Instructions and Manuals

A. Summary

A *set of instructions* is a process description written to enable a person to carry out a procedure safely and effectively. An effective set of instructions requires a very careful analysis of audience. The writer must determine how much the reader already knows about the activity itself and about related skills, equipment, and tools. A crucial point to remember in writing instructions is that most readers will not read the entire set of instructions before beginning; therefore, the writer must make sure that any necessary cautions or warnings are placed before the description of the step to which they pertain. The discussion of safety information covers writing it, designing it, and placing it in an appropriate location.

Instructions generally follow the same three-part structure used in mechanism and process descriptions. The general introduction explains why the task should be performed (if the reason is not obvious), provides any warnings or safety measures that concern the whole set of instructions, and describes or lists the tools and equipment that will be needed. Each step is written in the imperative mood and is sufficiently brief that the reader can perform the step without having to refer back to the instructions. Many kinds of instructions conclude with a troubleshooter's checklist, a table that helps the reader identify and solve common problems after the task has been completed.

A *manual* is an extensive set of instructions, often bound into a book. Manuals can be classified according to function: procedures, reference, maintenance, and so forth. The writing process used in most tech comm applies to the writing of manuals. One chief difference is that manuals are generally written collaboratively because of their size and complexity. As is the case with instructions, writers must analyze audience and purpose carefully. The front matter of a manual generally contains a cover, title page, table of contents, preface, conventions, and how-to-use-this-manual section. The body is structured according to how it will be used. The writing is simple and straightforward, with instructions written in the imperative. Graphics are plentiful. The back matter often consists of a glossary and an index.

This chapter also discusses writing instructions and manuals for nonnative speakers.

B. Goals

By the end of the chapter, students should be able to do the following:

1. describe the role of instructions and manuals in the workplace
2. explain the importance of assessing audience when writing instructions and manuals
3. write clear safety information
4. introduce and conclude instructions effectively

5. write clear and accurate step-by-step instructions
6. write effective front and back matter for manuals
7. organize the body of a manual according to how the reader will use it

C. Teaching Guide

A good set of instructions enables the audience to carry out the task effectively and safely. The writer is, of course, an inappropriate person to judge that effectiveness. If at all possible, have selected members of the class carry out the instructions written by other students. This is not as difficult as it might sound. For example, a good topic for a set of instructions is how to use a portable radio/cassette recorder to make an audiotape of a radio broadcast. There will surely be some students in every class who are unfamiliar with the process; they would make a perfect audience for a student who is writing the instructions. Nothing shows the writer the deficiencies of the description quite as effectively as witnessing another person fumble with a simple radio/cassette recorder.

Many aspects of the set of instructions can, of course, be analyzed in the traditional way: by looking carefully at the instructions themselves without trying to perform the task they describe. Among the most common problems are the following: the writer has failed to explain why the task should be carried out; the writer has not described all the necessary tools and equipment; the safety warnings and other comments follow, rather than precede, the pertinent steps; the steps themselves are not consistently numbered and expressed in the imperative mood; the steps contain either too much or too little information; and the writer has failed to include appropriate graphics that would simplify the instructions.

Your students probably will not have enough time to write a manual, but they will be able to write the front matter and a section of the body. Emphasize that the subject matter need not be particularly technical.

Traditional-Classroom Approaches

1. Additional Exercise: Brainstorming a Set of Instructions (see TechComm Web) asks students to practice the process of planning and drafting effective instructions. (25 minutes)
2. Additional Exercise: Analyzing a Humorous Manual invites students to consider the role of humor in instructions. You will need to print copies of a few sample pages. (15 minutes)
3. Ask students to describe the last time they learned how to use a new software application (or feature). Next, have them share which method of learning they prefer (oral instructions, trial and error, read instructions, watch as someone else performs skills, and so on) and then ask them what implications the discussion has for designing instructions. (35 minutes)
4. Provide sample passages from two sets of instructions with different approaches (one might be humorous or casual while the other might be just-the-facts or serious) and ask students to characterize the approaches. Have them describe which features of the writing and design contribute to their characterization. (25 minutes)
5. Provide sample safety information (manuals for consumer products are good sources) and have students evaluate the samples based on the guidelines discussed in the chapter. (20 minutes)

Technology-Enhanced Approaches

1. Additional Exercise: Describing Step-by-Step Instructions in a Manual invites students to describe the techniques used by writers to make a manual easy to use and understand. (30 minutes)

2. Additional Exercise: Evaluating a Set of Instructions asks students to use the Revision Checklist for instructions (page 543) to evaluate the effectiveness of an excerpt. (15 minutes)
3. Additional Project: Evaluating Instructions for Folding Attic Stairs asks students to review a set of instructions, paying particular attention to the integration of graphics and text, the legibility of the safety information, and the amount of information contained in each numbered step of the instructions. (25 minutes)
4. Ask students to learn a new feature on a word processor using the online help. Afterwards have them evaluate the effectiveness of the help and discuss the reactions they had while following the instructions. (30 minutes)

D. Suggestions for Responding to the Interactive Sample Document in the Book
For an additional Interactive Sample Document for Chapter 20, see TechComm Web.

1. How has the designer tried to ensure that readers will follow the steps in the correct order?

The designer has numbered the steps and used a strong vertical rule between the two columns to help readers follow the steps in the correct order.

2. Is the amount of information presented in each step appropriate?

Yes, each step contains an appropriate amount of information. For several steps, additional hints are presented in a smaller typeface.

3. What kind of information is presented in the imperative mood? What kind of information is not?

The only information not in the imperative is the note attached to step 2, because it is truly a note, not an action to be carried out.

4. How effectively are graphics used to support the textual information on this page?

The graphics—exploded diagrams with arrows showing actions—are effective because they do not overwhelm the reader with unnecessary information.

E. Suggestions for Responding to the Exercises, Projects, and Cases in the Book
Exercise 1. Although responses will vary, successful responses evaluate the introduction, step-by-step instructions, and conclusion. Many students successfully use the Revision Checklist (page 543) for this exercise.

Exercise 2. This set of instructions is ineffective. Most important, it fails to provide safety advice. It offers no warnings about proper use of tools or the need for safety glasses when sawing (step 2). The graphics in steps 2 and 8 show a person doing very dangerous things: leaning on a tub while sawing, and lifting heavy glass panels without a helper. In addition, the instructions are very unclear. There is no clear introduction that includes a list of materials, tools, and safety information. The step-by-step instructions are poorly written. For instance, in step 1, the writer does not explain how to use the tape correctly. In step 3, the writer presents information out of order. The graphics in step 7 are incomprehensible because they are not labeled correctly. There are many more problems with this set of instructions, enough for each student to list a different one if you discuss it in class.

Project 3. Responses will vary. I tell students when I assign this project that I will use the Revision Checklist (page 543) to evaluate their responses.

Project 4. Responses will vary. This project emphasizes the importance of having a representative sample of the audience test instructions as part of the revision process.

Case: Writing a Set of Instructions
The key to this assignment is the statement of audience: "Then write a clear set of instructions for someone who knows how to operate a computer but has not downloaded and installed software." Many people who use computers regularly have never downloaded, installed, and configured a program. Successful responses to this assignment will explain how to choose where to store the new file that is being downloaded, how to choose either a standard installation or a custom installation, how to decide where to put the new program as it installs, and one or more aspects of configuring the program once it is installed.

Chapter 21. Creating Web Sites

A. Summary

The process of creating a Web site begins like any other sort of tech-comm process: with analyzing audience and purpose. Web creators need to understand who their users are and what they want the site to do (for example, provide information, advertise products, or direct users to additional sources of information). Next, the Web creator needs to design the site and its pages. To a large degree, the design will depend on the analysis of audience and purpose. If, for example, users need to print the contents of the site, the Web creator will want to design it so that it is easy and economical to print. Then the Web creator must create and code the content for the site, not merely attach HTML codes to printed information and dump it on the site. The Web creator needs to revise and test the site, making sure that it meets the users' needs and that all its elements work correctly. The Web creator then launches the site on the Internet (or an intranet), registers it with search engines so users will be able to find it, and maintains the site periodically to keep users coming back.

An effective site design is simple: conservative backgrounds, good contrast between text and background, no decorative graphics, and thumbnail graphics instead of large ones. The text should be concise and simple, with good chunking. The pages should have clear, informative headers and footers. To make the site easy to navigate, it should include a site map, a table of contents at the top of long pages, back-to-top links, links to the home page, and redundant textual links. Sentences containing links should be written smoothly, as if the links do not appear, and should indicate what information the linked page contains. Links should use standard colors. Web clichés, such as "Check it out," are inappropriate. The site should be designed with features for people with vision, hearing, or motion impairments, as well as for multicultural users.

Issues of intellectual property for Web documents are still in legal flux, but all material on the Web is covered by U.S. copyright law, just like other documents.

B. Goals

By the end of the chapter, students should be able to do the following:

1. describe the process for creating Web sites
2. design an effective structure for a basic site
3. list the three techniques for coding material for use on the Web
4. apply effectively the seven design principles discussed in the chapter to create or evaluate a site and its pages

5. explain techniques for designing sites for readers with disabilities
6. explain techniques for designing sites for multicultural readers
7. discuss ethics and copyright law as they relate to the Web

C. Teaching Guide

With the passing of each semester, the number of students who have already made a Web site increases, and the number of students who are anxious about creating one decreases. Therefore, the amount of time you need to spend explaining basic coding is decreasing. Still, many students who have created Web sites need to understand the difference between sites meant to entertain and those meant to provide information. The typical student site violates many or even most of the principles explained in this chapter. The site might have ornate background images or red text against a purple background, annoying animation, large graphics, and no accommodation for people with slow modems, for people with disabilities, or for multicultural users.

In this way, your job is challenging in that some of your students need coaxing to even code a new paragraph, whereas others need to understand that they cannot include video and sound clips of their favorite music. I have found that making Web sites is an excellent collaborative assignment because the more-experienced students can help novices with basics, and the novices can help the more-experienced students with questions of design. Asking students with little or no Web design experience to complete the tutorial "Designing for the Web" (see TechComm Web) is an excellent method to help them quickly learn basic Web-design concepts.

Traditional-Classroom Approaches

Teaching Web-design principles in a traditional classroom is like teaching swimming without water—you can only accomplish so much before you need a pool or, in this case, the Internet. I recommend you reserve a computer lab for a few course meetings. However, the following activities do not require your students to have access to technology in the classroom.

1. Present a context for a Web site (for example, a site advertising a town's New Year's celebration) and have students sketch the basic structure of the site (see Figure 21.1, page 549). Ask students to compare their responses and discuss the similarities and differences. (30 minutes)
2. Provide students with several examples of ineffective links and ask them to revise them following the guidelines in the chapter. (15 minutes)
3. Give students a page of dense text from a technical document and ask them to revise it for the Web following the guidelines in the chapter. (20 minutes)
4. Distribute copies of screen captures of various sites and ask students to evaluate how well the pages help people with disabilities use the site. (20 minutes)
5. Ask students to share a recent experience they have had visiting a site for answers to specific questions, not for entertainment purposes. Use this discussion to emphasize the importance of audience and purpose when designing sites. (25 minutes)

Technology-Enhanced Approaches

1. Additional Exercise: Buying from a Spanish-Friendly Computer Manufacturer (see TechComm Web) invites students to consider Web design for a global audience. (25 minutes)
2. Additional Exercise: Determining Site-Registration Hurdles invites students to learn more about search engine policies for registering a site. (15 minutes)

3. Additional Exercise: Studying How to Write Graceful Links invites students to study the *Web Style Guide* for information about how links should be written and formatted. (15 minutes)
4. Additional Exercise: Identifying Poor Sites asks students to study really bad sites and discuss how they can "learn good design by looking at bad design." (20 minutes)
5. Additional Exercise: Is Cool Good? asks students to study "cool" sites and discuss whether a cool site is necessarily a well-designed site. (20 minutes)

D. Suggestions for Responding to the Interactive Sample Document in the Book
For an additional Interactive Sample Document for Chapter 21, see TechComm Web.

1. What is the audience for this site? Which elements of this page indicate its audience?

The audience for this site is primarily young people (see the large photo) interested in Web design (see the reference to the primer) and people potentially interested in hiring the Web designer (see the link to Feldman's portfolio).

2. What is the purpose of this site? Which elements of this page indicate its purpose?

The purposes of the site are to spread Feldman's reputation as a Web designer (see the primer and the "free creations") and to interest potential customers of his services (see the portfolio).

3. Evaluate the ease of navigation. How easy do you think it would be to find what you needed on this site?

The few links seem clear. Unclear, however, are the differences among "stuff," "portfolio," and "professional and personal projects."

4. Evaluate the integration of the links in the text window. How smoothly has the author integrated the links with the text?

The links are integrated very smoothly. See, for example, the sentence "Within these pages you will find many examples of my professional and personal projects."

E. Suggestions for Responding to the Exercises, Projects, and Cases in the Book
Exercise 1. Responses will vary. This exercise provides students with practice describing different features of sites, comparing design approaches, and evaluating the effectiveness of the design.

Exercise 2. Responses will vary. This exercise emphasizes the importance of a site's design to people with disabilities and introduces students to several of the ways they can make a site easier to use for people with disabilities.

Project 3. Responses will vary. I encourage students to not only consider the content of the site but also the design of the site and the effectiveness of the instructions (see Chapter 20).

Project 4. Although responses will vary, successful students are able not only to use principles and guidelines from this chapter to support their claims but also to use skills learned in earlier chapters to write and design their report effectively. Because students are part of the audience for their college's or university's Web site, they are able to readily identify strengths and weaknesses.

Case: Creating a Web Site
This case requires that students synthesize all the information in this chapter, from analyzing an audience and purpose to testing and revising the site they have created. The additional activities at the end—keeping a log and presenting an oral report on the process—encourage students to be self-reflective as they go through the different steps in creating and testing the site.

Chapter 22. Making Oral Presentations

A. Summary

This chapter discusses the extemporaneous and the scripted oral presentation. Although oral presentations can be expensive and inconvenient, they are necessary because they enable a dialogue between the speaker and the audience. Preparing to give an oral presentation requires five steps: analyzing the speaking situation, preparing an outline or note cards, preparing presentation graphics, choosing effective language, and rehearsing the presentation. The presentation graphics should help listeners understand the organization and development of the presentation and remember its key information. In giving the presentation, speakers should try to control five aspects of their voice: volume, speed, pitch, clarity of pronunciation, and verbal fillers. They should also try to maintain eye contact at all times and avoid distracting mannerisms. After the presentation, speakers should address the audience's questions.

B. Goals

By the end of the chapter, students should be able to do the following:

1. discuss the role of oral presentations in the workplace
2. list the four basic types of presentations
3. deliver a presentation designed for a specific audience and purpose
4. manage their time effectively during a presentation
5. select appropriate media for a presentation
6. design effective presentation graphics
7. use effective language
8. rehearse effectively
9. describe strategies to calm their nerves
10. describe strategies to use their voices and bodies effectively
11. discuss how to respond to common question-and-answer situations
12. evaluate an oral presentation

C. Teaching Guide

The only effective way to teach oral presentations, of course, is to have students give them. In tech-comm courses, there are many excellent opportunities for brief extemporaneous or scripted oral presentations: descriptions, instructions, proposals, and completion reports. The other students in the class act as the audience, and the student introduces the presentation by telling them who he or she is (in the context of the project) and who they are. The audience's role is crucial, for they are responsible for asking questions at the end of the presentation. A presentation in which the speaker has not made clear the problem motivating the project is seriously flawed. Even if the speaker has made the problem clear, he or she will gain valuable experience by responding politely to the questioner.

Another effective way to provide feedback to the speaker is to use an evaluation sheet that focuses on the mechanical aspects of the presentation (voice, eye contact, and so forth) and the informational aspects (specific to whatever assignment the speaker is fulfilling). Both you and the students should fill out these evaluation forms and give them to each speaker at the end of the presentation. Some teachers like to grade the student on the basis of everyone's evaluation form (although this inevitably leads to grade inflation on that assignment). Other teachers do not compute the audience's evaluations. (An evaluation sheet is included in the chapter and in the Forms for Technical Communication section on Tech Comm Web.) The tutorial "Preparing Presentation Slides," also on TechComm Web, is an excellent starting place for students unfamiliar with presentation-graphics software.

Traditional-Classroom Approaches

1. Additional Exercise: Evaluating Presentation-Graphics Templates (see TechComm Web) asks students to evaluate the design of Microsoft PowerPoint® templates. You will need to make transparencies or print copies of a few templates. (20 minutes)
2. Additional Project: Delivering an Impromptu Presentation requires students to plan, organize, and present a 5-minute presentation on a key word or concept from their major. (60 minutes)
3. Ask students to write 10 questions a general audience might ask about a topic the students feel confident talking about. In small groups, use these questions to conduct mock Q&A sessions. (40 minutes)
4. Distribute copies of the Oral Presentation Evaluation Form reproduced in the chapter (Figure 22.6, page 588) as well as several others (from the Internet or other courses) and ask students to discuss the strengths and limitations of each form. Conclude by having students design their own form, using the most effective elements from each form. (40 minutes)
5. Brainstorm a list of distracting mannerisms (for example, talking to the screen, excessive *uhms,* playing with the pointer, and so on) students have observed during presentations and discuss strategies for avoiding these behaviors. (20 minutes)

Technology-Enhanced Approaches

1. Additional Exercise: Poking Fun at Presentation-Graphics Software invites students to study a parody of presentation-graphics software. (15 minutes)
2. Additional Project: Creating Presentation Graphics for a Presentation asks students to create a set of presentation graphics in the form of bulleted text that might accompany a speech. (35 minutes)
3. Ask students to locate and listen to a presentation delivered entirely online. These presentations are often referred to as *webcasts.* Then ask students to describe the differences and similarities of webcasts and face-to-face presentations. (40 minutes)
4. Ask students to write five questions a general audience might ask about a topic the students feel confident talking about. In small groups, use these questions to conduct mock Q&A sessions in a synchronous or asynchronous online forum. Afterwards ask students to discuss the strengths and limitations of conducting a Q&A session online. (40 minutes)

D. Suggestions for Responding to the Interactive Sample Document in the Book
For an additional Interactive Sample Document for Chapter 22, see TechComm Web.

1. How effective is the contrast between the color of the text and the color of the background?

The contrast is good in some places and poor in others, improving as the blue background darkens. This background shows a limitation of using a graduated color.

2. What is the function of the graphic of the key?

The graphic has no obvious function. Because it is ineffective, it should be deleted.

3. What information would you add to the footer?

In addition to the slide number, the footer should include the name and date of the presentation.

4. What other changes would you make to the design of this slide?

I'd put the date of publication in parentheses after the number of the edition to cut down the number of lines displayed on the slide. I'd consider changing to a sans serif text, which is easier to read on screen. I'd also consider presenting the information in a table, rather than a list. Doing so would help the writer realize that he or she is not presenting information consistently for each of the three editions (the bullet list for the First Edition contains an extra item).

E. Suggestions for Responding to the Exercises, Projects, and Cases in the Book
Exercise 1. This exercise requires students to familiarize themselves with basic features of the presentation-graphics software available to them. The basic skills students learn from this exercise will help them when they have to deliver a presentation supported by graphics. I have found that some students in my courses are already familiar with presentation-graphics software and serve as excellent tutors to those students just learning the software.

Exercise 2. Responses will vary. This exercise shows students that design elements such as color and backgrounds do not work well when produced for back-and-white transparencies. One design consideration students often ignore is the fact that standard transparency machines project slides most effectively if they have a portrait orientation. On the other hand, slides with a landscape orientation work best for digital projectors.

Project 3. Responses will vary. This project is valuable because it provides students with practice speaking in front of an audience and gives them feedback from their audience. For those students in the audience, the presentations familiarize them with the evaluation form and give them practice evaluating a presentation.

Project 4. Responses will vary. This project serves as good opportunity to include an oral-presentation component in the students' major assignment sequence for the course (proposal, progress report, completion or research report, and oral presentation).

Case: Identifying Resources for Students in Your Major
This case calls for students to synthesize all the information in this chapter. They have been given an audience and purpose, but they need to generate the information, select an appropriate organizational pattern, create the slides, rehearse the presentation, and deliver it.